MAŁGORZATA MIRGA-TAS

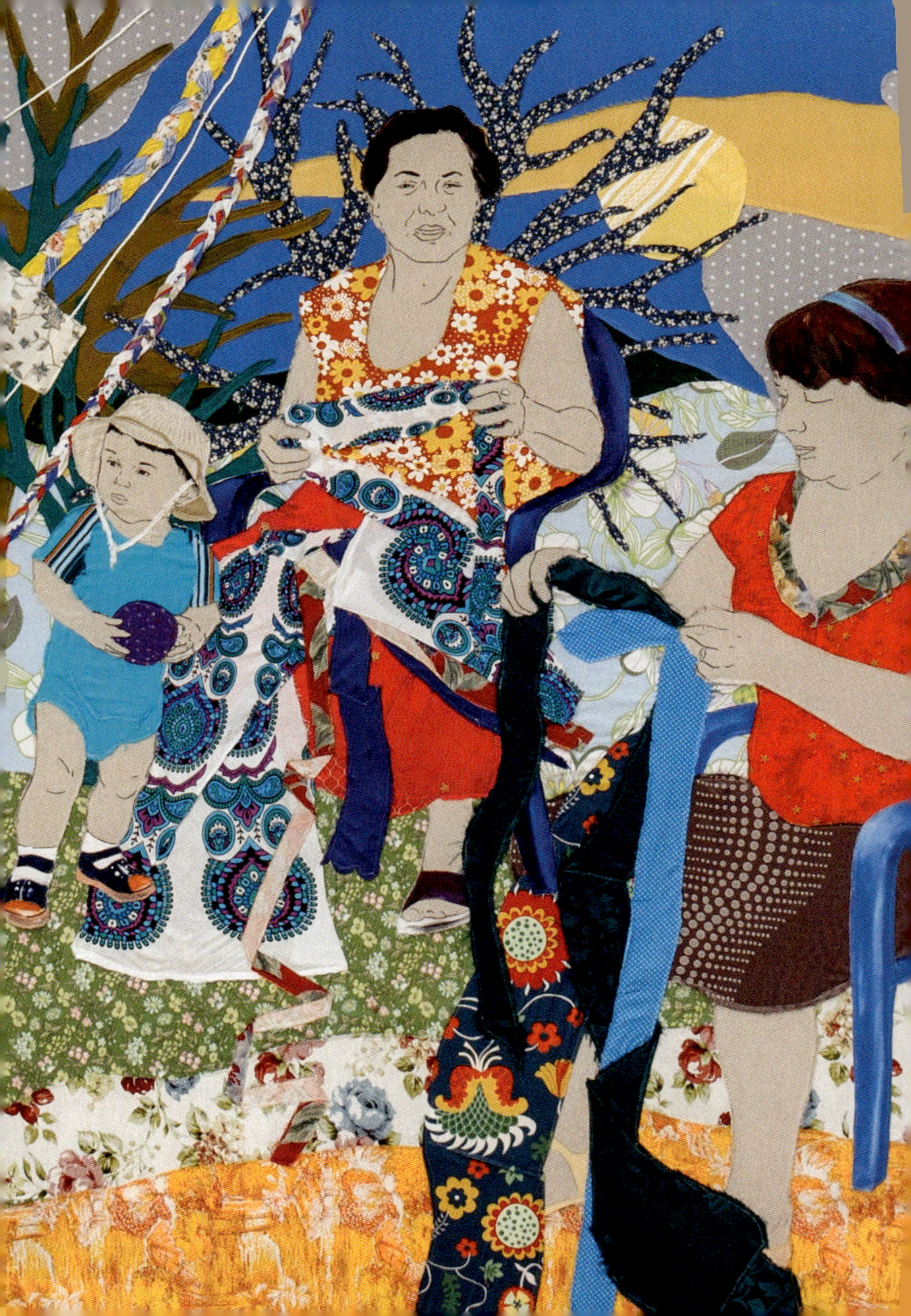

MAŁGORZATA MIRGA-TAS

EDITED BY ANNE BARLOW & GILES JACKSON

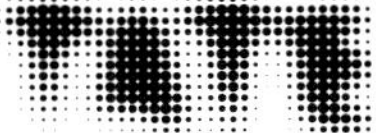

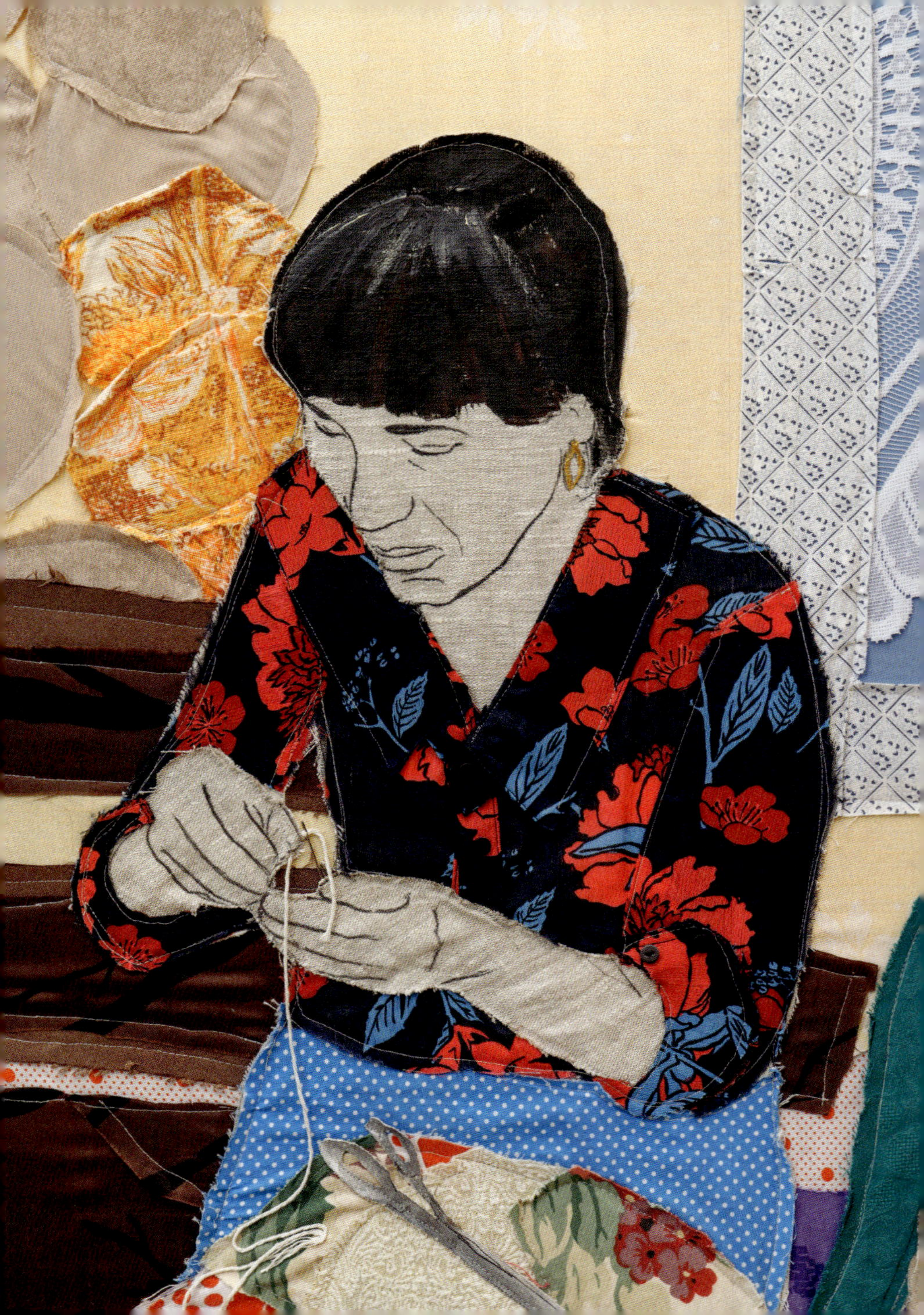

CONTENTS

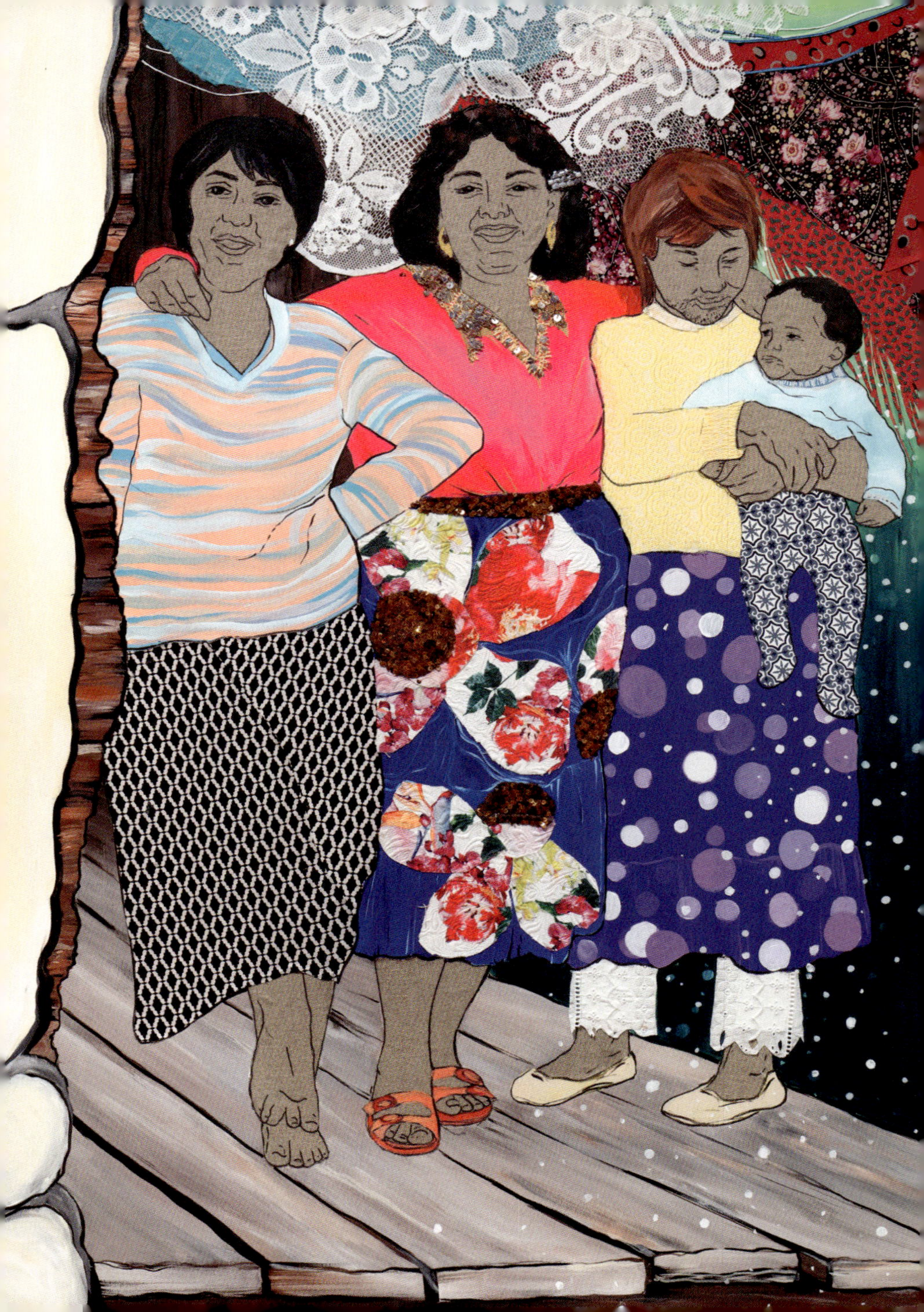

PREFACE

Anne Barlow

Małgorzata Mirga-Tas (b.1978) is a Polish Romani visual artist, educator and activist based in the community of Bergitka Roma in the village of Czarna Góra in the Tatra Mountains, southern Poland. Initially trained as a sculptor, she is primarily known for her vibrant textile collages that challenge stereotypical representations of Romani people. Often working in collaboration with other women, Mirga-Tas sews together pieces of clothing, tablecloths, curtains and sheets to create vivid portraits and scenes from everyday life.

This book includes significant recent works as well as new textile pieces created in 2024 especially for the exhibition at Tate St Ives: *Kovaci (Blacksmiths)* (pp.38–41), *Roma Pasio Peskro Khier (Roma in Front of the House)* (pp.35–7), *Still on the Journey* (pp.54–9), *Dromeskri zuta (On the Journey)* (pp.48–53), *Romani Kali Daj (Roma Madonna)* (p.12) and *Ćhajengri Duma (Women's Thoughts)* (p.13). The show also presents for the first time three works recently acquired for Tate's collection: *Miri Daj (My Mother)* (pp.22–3) and *Side Thawenca (Sewn with Threads)* 2019 (pp.24–5), and *The Three Graces* 2021 (opposite). From portraits of individuals to narratives on a monumental scale, the works here collectively present affirmative images of Romani identity, imbued with strength and dignity.

As curator and art historian Timea Junghaus observes in her essay for this publication (pp.15–21), such Roma-led perspectives are critically important in addressing and challenging stereotypes that have existed across the centuries and are still pervasive today. Junghaus describes Mirga-Tas as 'an active shaper of the Romani cultural movement, a storyteller of Romani resistance, who unveils and liberates the still invisible and oppressed Romani histories and genealogy in Europe.' She refers to the many distinctive features of Mirga-Tas's practice, from the feminist perspective that informs her work to her commitment to future generations of Romani communities – citing her founding of Foundation Jaw Dikh!, one of the first artist residencies in Europe to create opportunities for transnational dialogue primarily among Romani artists.

Both Junghaus and the artist Katarzyna Depta-Garapich note the importance in Romani culture of the interdependence between humans and non-humans – as often visualised in Mirga-Tas's depictions of people in landscapes alongside animals including horses, cats, dogs and chickens. In her text

The Three Graces 2021
Acrylic paint and fabrics
on canvas
150.2 × 112.3

(pp.32–3), Depta-Garapich explores the special significance of the bear to Romani culture in terms of its animistic and mythological associations, and considers the ways in which the bear is represented in her own and Mirga-Tas's work. In her essay, curator, writer and educator Övül Ö. Durmuşoğlu emphasises the female-centred perspectives in Mirga-Tas's work, as seen in the *Herstories* project 2019–21 for the third Autostrada Biennale in Prizren, Kosovo, which featured large-scale portraits of Romani women on the exteriors of buildings in the city (pp.60–3). Considering other works sited in outdoor spaces, Durmuşoğlu refers to a carved wooden memorial that Mirga-Tas originally made to honour twenty-nine Romani people murdered in 1942 during the Second World War – a monument subsequently destroyed in an act of anti-Roma violence – and *Wesiune Thana* (*Place in the Woods*) 2016, an intervention that the artist carried out onto Romani houses in an open-air museum of rural culture. In citing these examples, Durmuşoğlu points to the social and political importance of such works in asserting female authorship, memorialising victims of violence and challenging museological representations of Romani communities. Both of these works are discussed in greater detail in the conversation with the artist later in the book (pp.74–91).

This challenging of stereotypes is addressed by curator and writer Wojciech Szymański specifically in relation to Mirga-Tas's approach to art historical representations of Romani identity (pp.42–7). In his text, Szymański mentions the significance of the installation *Atlas*, presented within the exhibition *Travelling Images* (2022) at the International Cultural Centre in Kraków, which comprised images of Romani people spanning more than five centuries. Szymański refers to these images, all of which were created by non-Romani artists, as a form of 'visual colonisation' of Romani culture that Mirga-Tas actively seeks to address. In particular, he highlights a series of prints by the Lorraine painter Jacques Callot, *The Gypsies* 1621–31, elsewhere called *Life of the Egyptians*, which Mirga-Tas subsequently reappropriated and reclaimed in her joyous, large-format textiles entitled *Out of Egypt* 2021 (p.43).

This is Mirga-Tas's first institutional exhibition in the UK and we are delighted that it will be adapted for presentation at the Whitworth, The University of Manchester in spring 2025. There it will be shown in the context of the Whitworth's rich collections of textiles and embroidery, spanning local production and items from communities across the globe, both recent and historical. We are extremely grateful to the artist, museums and private collectors who so generously lent their works to the show. We would like to thank The Małgorzata Mirga-Tas Exhibition Supporters Circle: The Polish Cultural Institute in London and Frith Street Gallery, London, and all Tate Members for their generous support.

For their insightful new texts on Mirga-Tas featured in this publication, we would like to thank Katarzyna Depta-Garapich, Övül Ö. Durmuşoğlu, Timea Junghaus and Wojciech Szymański. We would also like to acknowledge all the Tate staff who have made this project possible, especially Giles Jackson, Helen Bent, Louise Connell, Luke Walder and the wider Programming, Technical and Conservation teams. In addition, we extend thanks to colleagues at the Whitworth: Sook-Kyung Lee, Darren Pih, Valentin Diakonov, Victoria Hartley and their supporting teams. Above all, we are enormously grateful to Małgorzata Mirga-Tas for sharing with us her powerful and unique artistic vision.

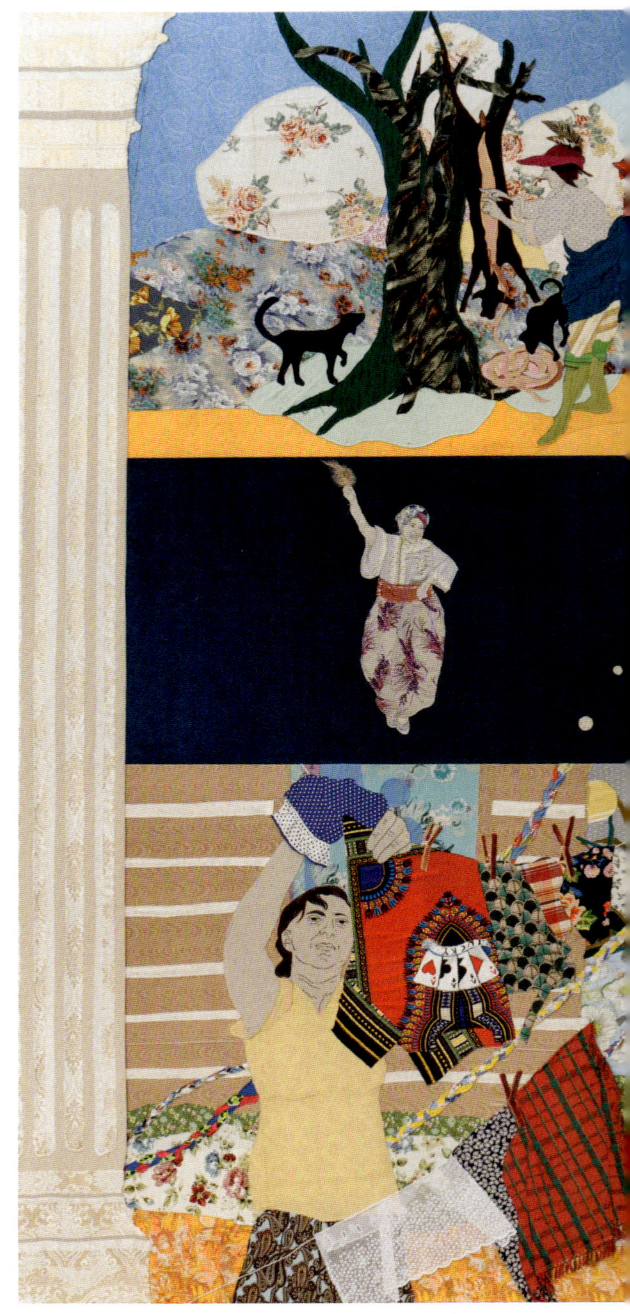

June 2022 from
Re-enchanting the World
Acrylic paint and fabrics
on canvas
462 × 541 × 7

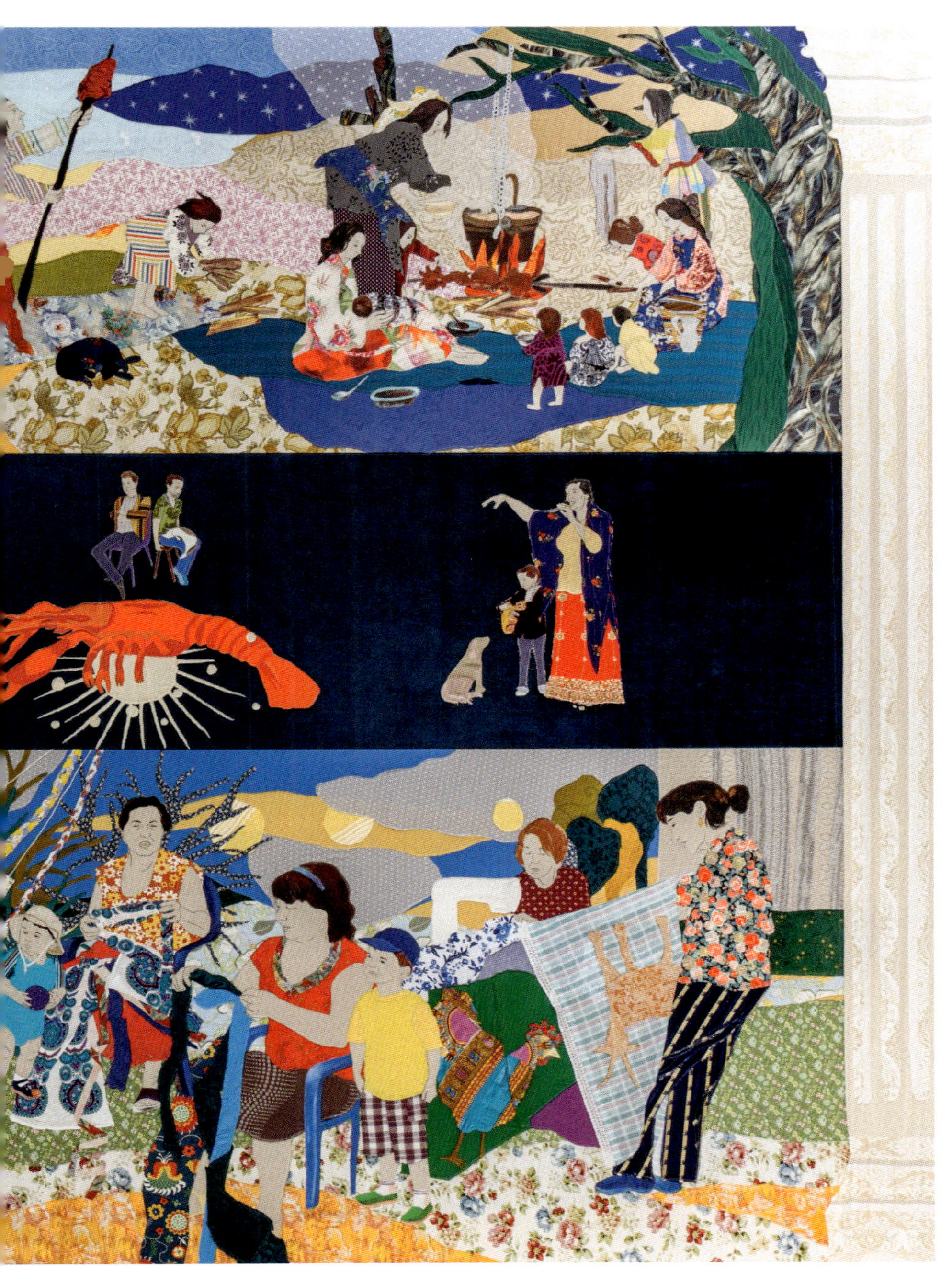

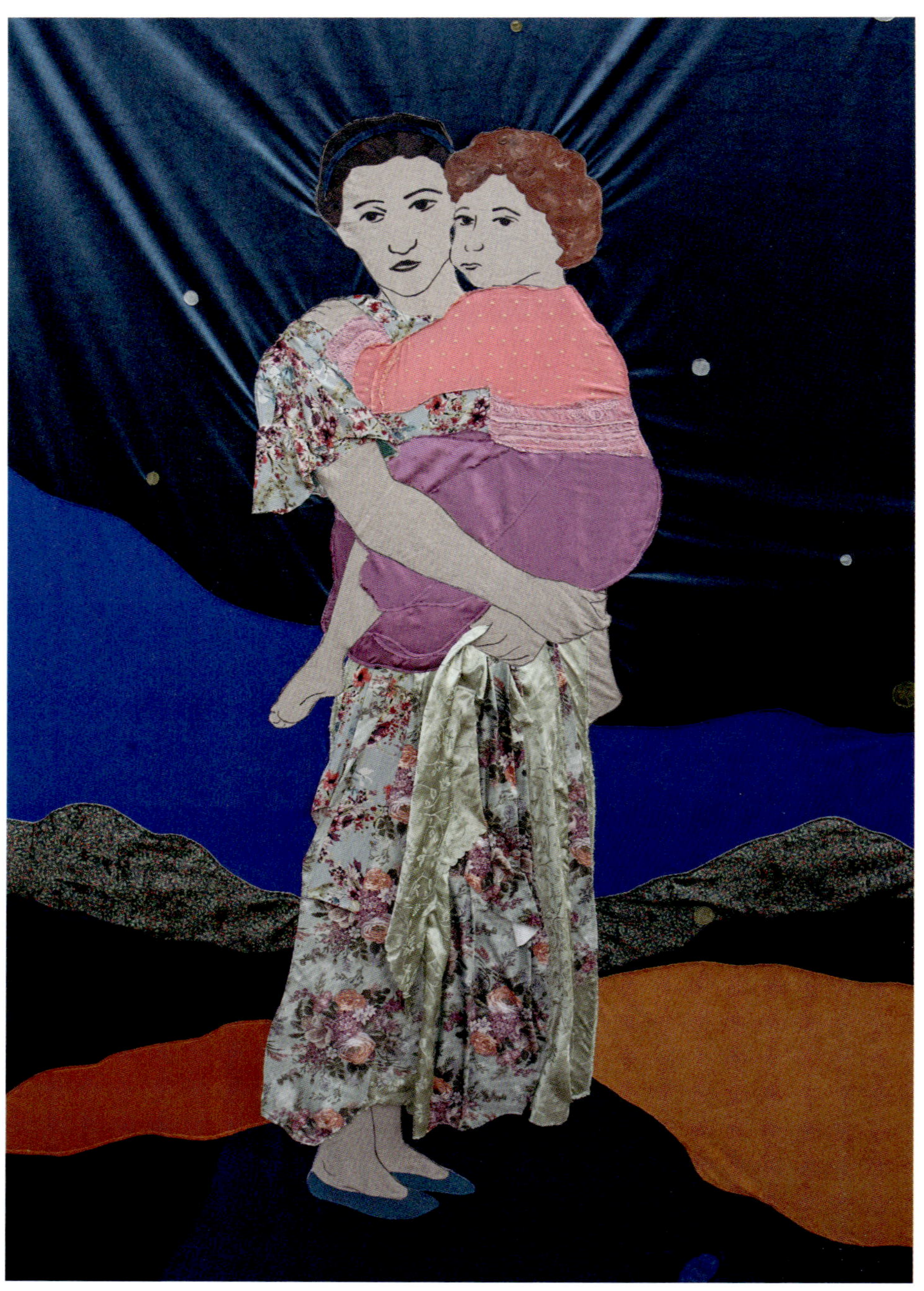

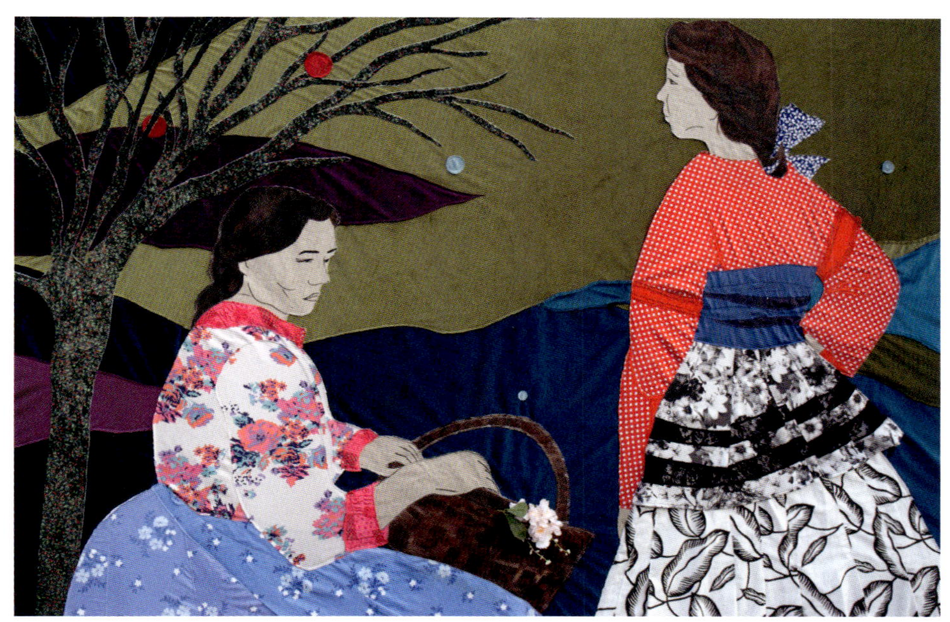

In-progress view of *Romani
Kali Daj (Roma Madonna)*
(detail) 2024
Acrylic paint and fabrics
on canvas
462 × 280 × 7

In-progress view of
*Ćhajengri Duma (Women's
Thoughts)* (detail) 2024
Acrylic paint and fabrics
on canvas
462 × 300 × 7

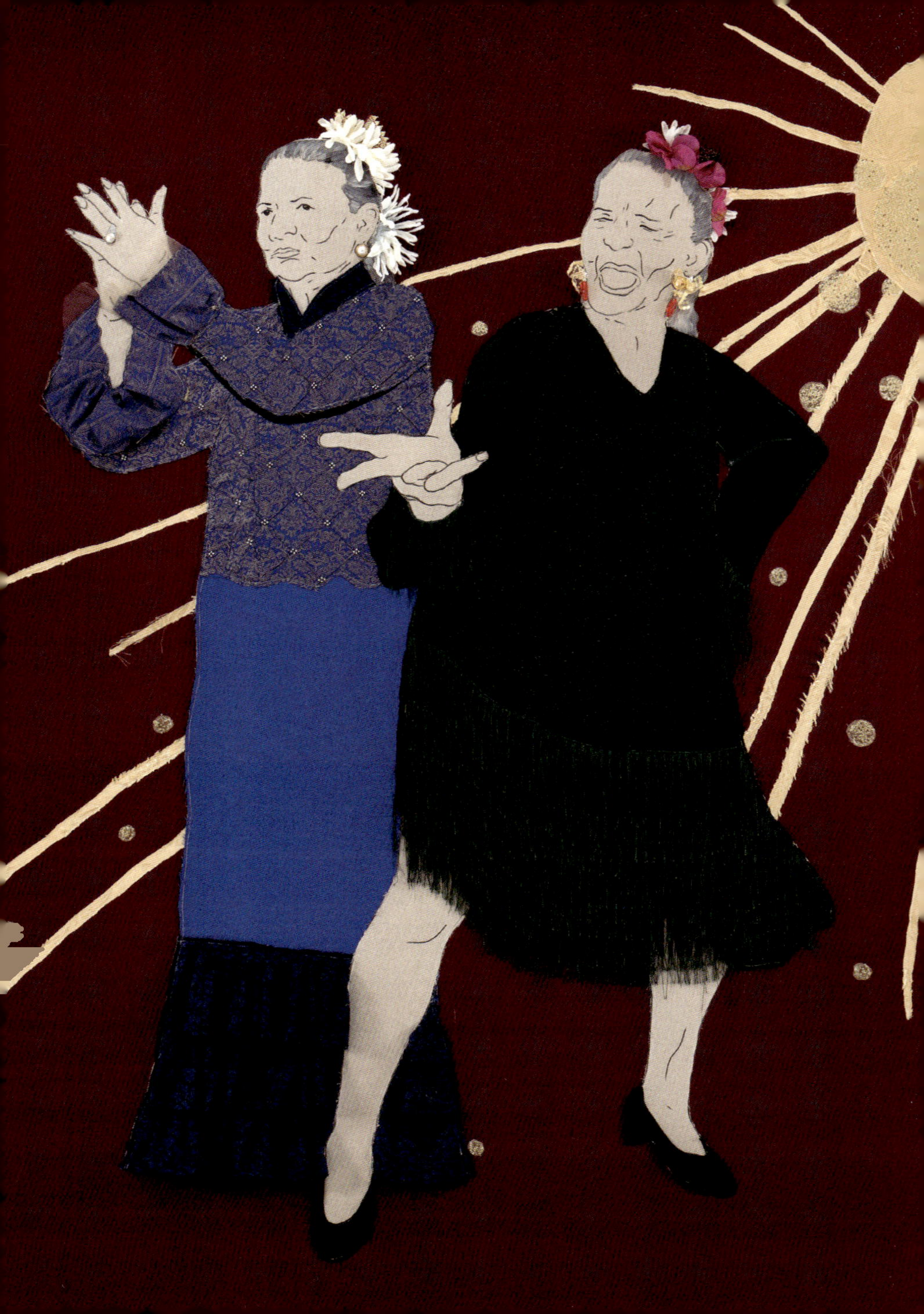

MAKING OURSELVES ANEW

Timea Junghaus

We Romani claim the art of Małgorzata Mirga-Tas as a groundbreaking and historic achievement in Romani history. For artists and intellectuals, stating one's Romani identity is always a double-edged sword. As an educated contemporary artist who completed her fine arts education at the prestigious Academy of Fine Arts in Kraków, Poland, Mirga-Tas has had many opportunities to leave her Romani identity behind – yet she has never had an issue with being called a 'Romani artist'. Indeed, she embraces it.

Małgorzata Mirga-Tas was raised in the community of Bergitka Roma in Czarna Góra near Zakopane, in the Tatra Mountains of Poland, where she continues to live. She is a transformational activist for the importance of creating contemporary artistic strategies for the transfer of the memory of the Roma Holocaust to the next generations: the organisation she founded, Foundation Jaw Dikh!, was one of the first in Europe to arrange artists' camps for nurturing a transnational exchange and belonging among Romani artists. She is an active shaper of the Romani cultural movement, a storyteller of Romani resistance, who unveils and liberates the still invisible and oppressed histories and genealogy of the Roma in Europe.

A central aspect of Mirga-Tas's art is built on the ancient Romani knowledge of how to repair and create beauty and to make art where others see only waste and objects that have been discarded and rejected: her textiles are collages and patchworks that recycle clothing and shiny decorative objects into large, colourful narrative panels. Her work involves a radical reimagining of the most significant notions that define our lives, such as belonging, home, nation and history. In this, her art is specifically Romani, yet unusually global. It invites universal participation.

Since 2020, Mirga-Tas has exhibited in the most prestigious of art events. In 2022, she became the first Romani artist ever selected to represent a national pavilion in the Giardini of the Biennale. Her installation for the Polish Pavilion, *Re-enchanting the World* (pp.10–11, 17), took inspiration from the historical frescoes of Palazzo Schifanoia in Ferrara, Italy (p.16). In this artwork, she created historical portraiture, depicting Romani leaders past and present – the majority of them women – together with scenes of the life of her local and transnational community. She has also presented at Documenta xv in Kassel (2022), contributed to the *Barvalo* exhibition at the Musée des

*Herminia Borja 2023
(detail, see p.66)
Acrylic paint and
fabrics on canvas
265.5 × 323*

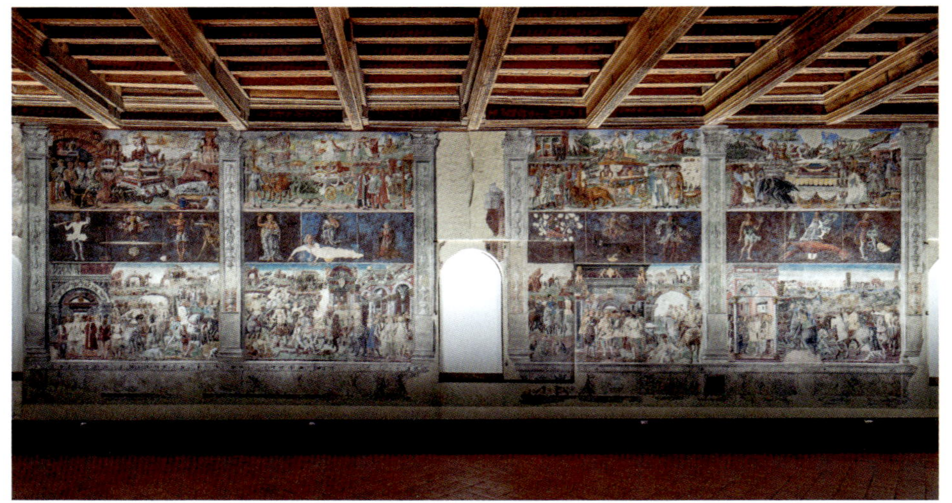

Detail of the fifteenth-century fresco paintings in the Palazzo Schifanoia in Ferrara, Italy. Known as *The Hall of the Months*, these monumental wall paintings represent the twelve months of the year, and their accompanying signs of the zodiac. From the Zachęta – National Gallery of Art archives

OPPOSITE
Re-enchanting the World 2022
Acrylic paint and fabrics on canvas
Dimensions variable
Installation at the 59th Venice Biennale
See also pp.10–11 and 46–7

civilisations de l'Europe (Mucem) in Marseille (May–September 2023), and presented monographic exhibitions in Białystok, Berlin and Seville (June–September 2023, February–March 2021 and September 2023–March 2024 respectively). She won Polityka's Passport award for best Polish artist in 2020 and, a year later, the Tajsa Roma Cultural Heritage Prize, proving her acceptance and celebration by both the Polish and the 'Roma nation'. In 2024 Mirga-Tas became the first artist of Romani heritage to have her works enter Tate's collection, with her solo show at Tate St Ives featuring a selection of her most defining artworks of recent years, complemented by new works created for the exhibition. And so her star continues to rise.

Throughout her artistic career, Mirga-Tas has shed light on the workings of stereotyping, and developed a sensitive representation mode and technique to offer a contrastingly respectful and political representation of the Romani people.

The Romani stereotype is enacted in the moment of the gaze. Romani bodies are relegated to an underclass in a historical construct that has multiple origins. The imaginarium which condenses the Roma into the iconography of the stranger, pagan, alien, thief, evil and ugly, had already developed by the fifteenth and sixteenth centuries (in Northern Renaissance art); since then, the history of the over six hundred years of Romani enslavement (in the former territories of Romania) has remained untaught and largely unknown in Europe. In the Eastern, Central

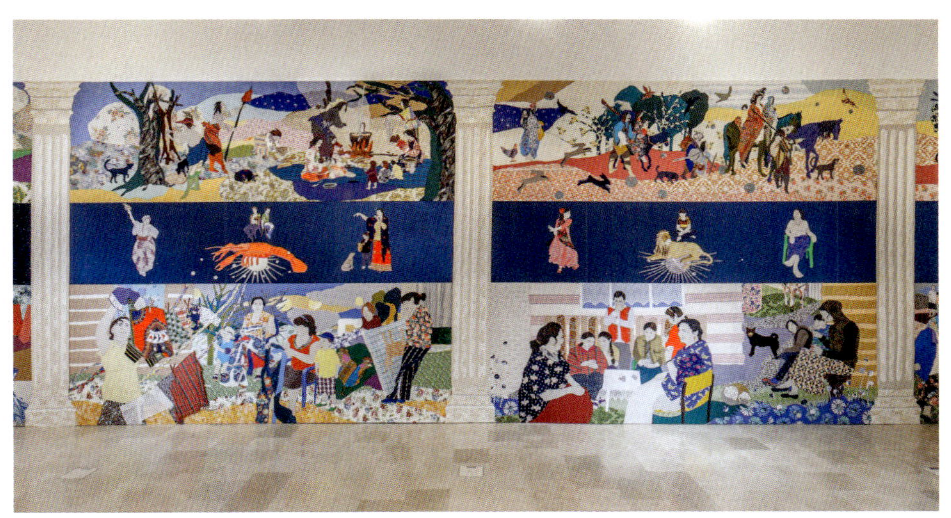

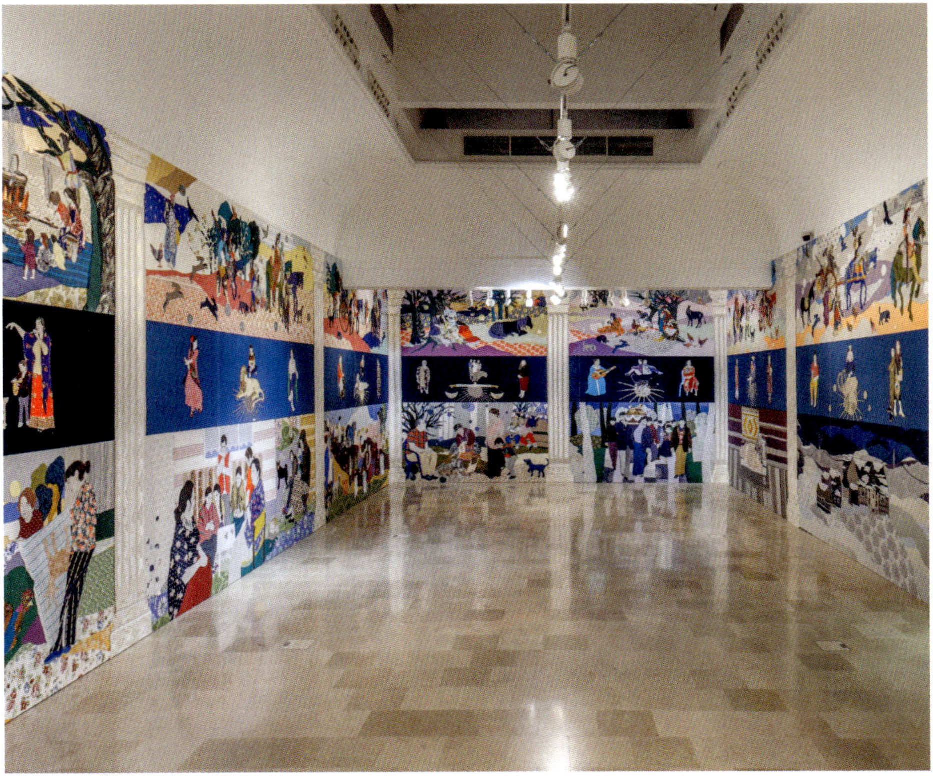

and Southern-European panoptic regime of modernity,
Romani people became the pendants of Western Europe's
African and Asian 'primitives', and the Romani body, like
the Black body, was criminalised, sexualised and feminised.[1]
This burden of being the 'other' – and the physical, symbolic,
epistemic violence towards the Roma – culminated in the
murder of more than 500,000 in the Second World War. The
Roma Holocaust was only officially recognised in 1982 when
German Chancellor Helmut Schmidt publicly stated that the
persecution of the Roma between 1939 and 1945 'for reasons
of race' was, on the level of international law, a genocide.[2]

This history of 'othering' complicates social relations
because of how it is inextricably woven into the European
collective consciousness and the European cultural ethos
through art and popular media. Unlike the spectatorship
and surveillance that characterises much of the depiction of
Romani people throughout history, Mirga-Tas's is an insider's
view. She shows ordinary Roma – primarily Romani women –
living their everyday lives: sitting outside, doing housework,
tending to children, drinking coffee together, participating in

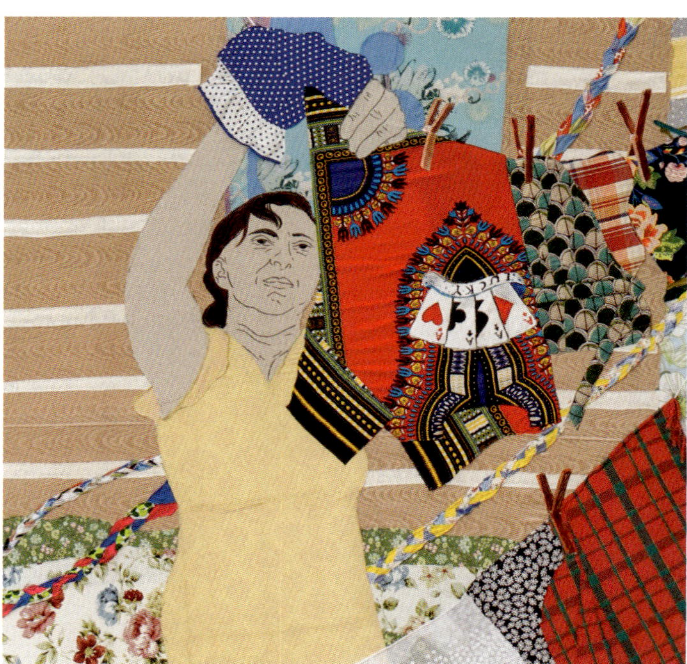

Details of the panel
June from *Re-enchanting
the World* 2022. See also
pp.10–11

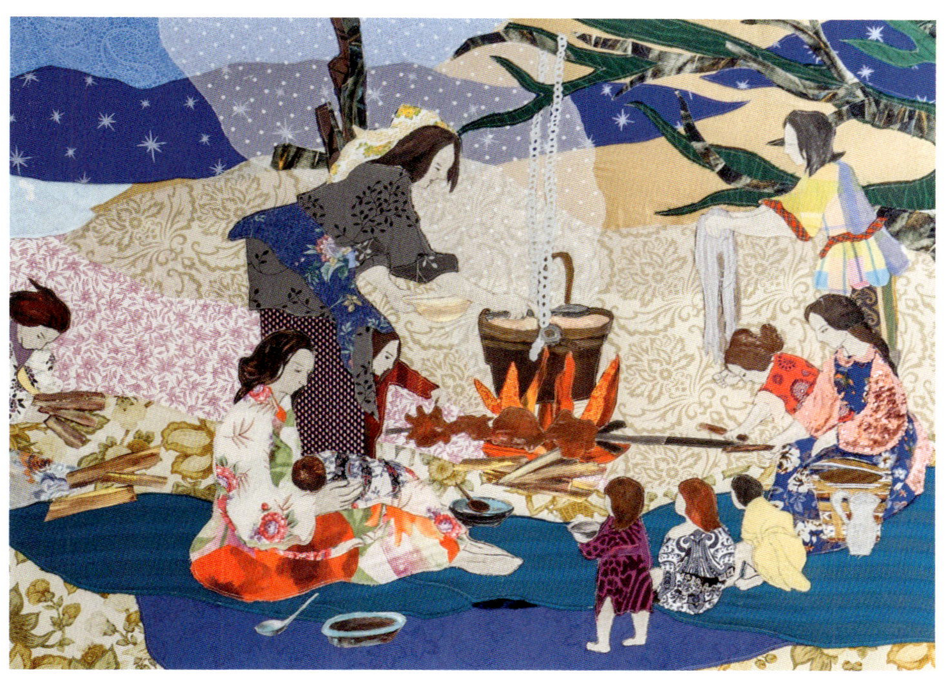

family or community assemblies. The ordinary act of coming together and building bonds, relationships and friendships is the focus of her attention. In her large, soft, colourful textiles, she demonstrates the Romani community's reinvention of the notion of home: for us, home is not a fenced-off private property but an extended understanding of human relations and connection rituals for bonding. This is how we Romani have always been able to repair our homes and our sense of security even in the face of violence, genocide and evictions targeting our communities in Europe.

As an outspoken feminist, Mirga-Tas pays distinct attention to the political aspect of women's assemblies. In her textiles we see women, friends or relatives of multiple generations sitting around the coffee table or in a public space. Their bodies coming together, their conversations tuning in together and their shared rituals give the impression of gossip. As feminist theorist Silvia Federici notes: 'In early modern England, the word "gossip" referred to companions in childbirth not limited to the midwife. It also became a term for women's friends, with no necessary derogatory connotations. In either case, it had strong emotional connotations.'[3] This connection between women and its potential to 'repair' and heal is central to Mirga-Tas's art.

In her larger narrative textiles and portraits, Mirga-Tas contemplates the Romani nation. Through the use of discourse, stories, images, events and objects, she posits a transgressive extraterritorial political identity: an identification with an imagined common entity based on an 'us' unlimited by borders and scattered in diasporic spaces. In this vision, the Roma-transgressed nation is our community and our belonging: a nation that is parallel to and aware of other transnational movements, and is inspired by the transnational feminist movement, the notions of the creolised, border gnosis, third space and dissemination, and other subaltern discourses.

Mirga-Tas unlearns the European history that was 'taught to us', in which Romani people do not exist. She sews, stitches and patches together a new (her)story. Her hard labour delivers a new understanding, where beautiful and often monumental brown-skinned figures contribute with their lives and resources to a Europe where we are all allowed to live in peaceful cohabitation.

The hope Mirga-Tas's work embodies and conveys is undoubtedly increasingly important in today's Europe of resurgent racism, economic crisis and uncertainties, and the growing number of paramilitary organisations, racist and neo-Nazi groups and nationalist formations. Against this ominous backdrop, Mirga-Tas's artworks show Romani people complete in their dignity, and worthy of respect. More importantly, her artistic strategy transfers to new generations a knowledge of Romani traditions and rituals, and the Romani people's own understanding of our entangled history, the planet and the universe. She demonstrates the importance of living in connection with the animal and natural world, with horses, cats, dogs and chickens often the companions of the people she depicts, while plants, herbs, the mountain and the forest appear in the background or as decoration, and are often shown in the context of beautifying or healing, in tea-making or cooking, for example. Repetition, momentum and rhythm are also important to her paintings: she will often continue a pattern of decorations (beads, spangles, ribbons) or ornamental motifs simply to enjoy their rhythm, just as we do in our songs and music. In this way, Mirga-Tas's art, and art by other contemporary artists of Romani heritage, has been the most efficient vehicle for the exploration of Romani subjectivities over the past decades.

'Opposition', writes the African-American feminist critic bell hooks, 'is not enough. In the vacant space after one has resisted there is still the necessity to become – to make oneself anew.'[4] It is in this work of 'making ourselves anew' that Romani artists find their most vital and defining role. Mirga-Tas is adept at navigating the irony, incongruity and complexity of Romani life, but also the fertility and pride contained in the concept of being Romani. She gives it form. She embodies it. She thrives.

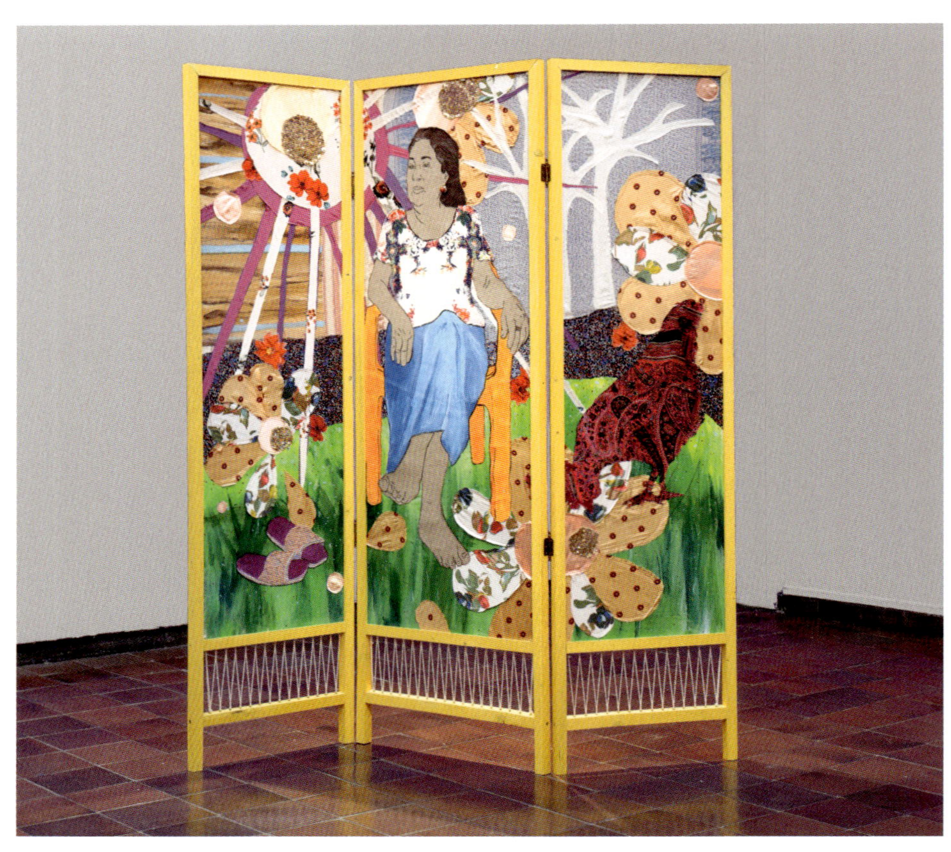

Miri Daj (My Mother) 2019
Acrylic paint and fabrics on
wooden screen
186 × 161

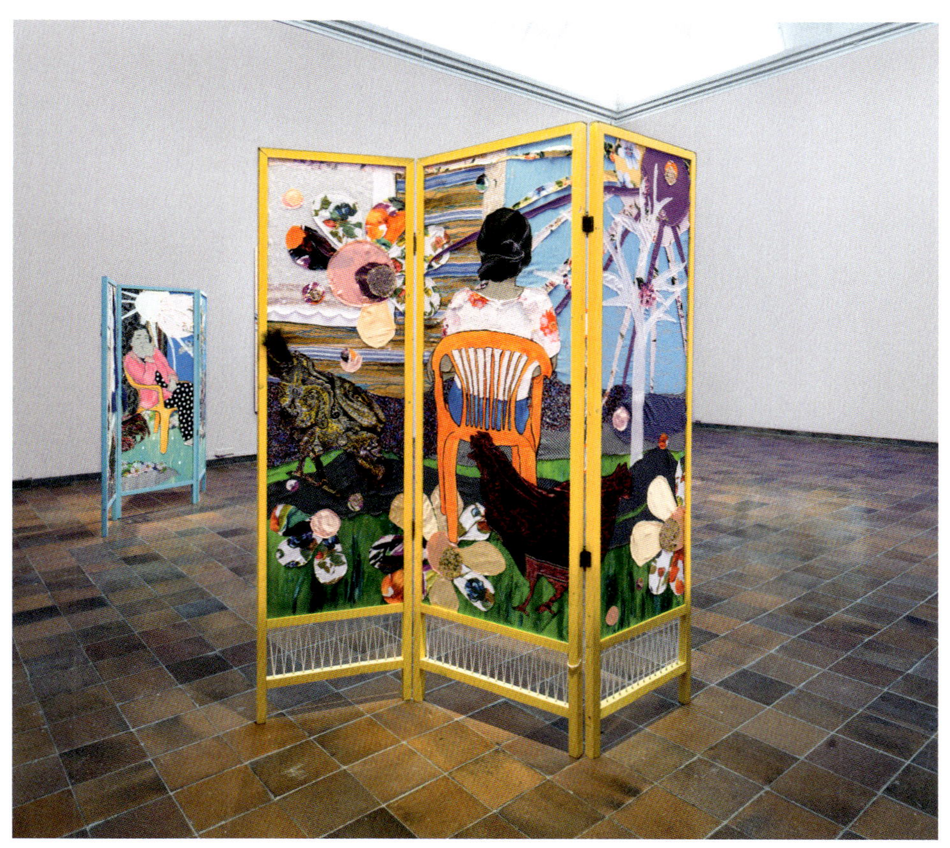

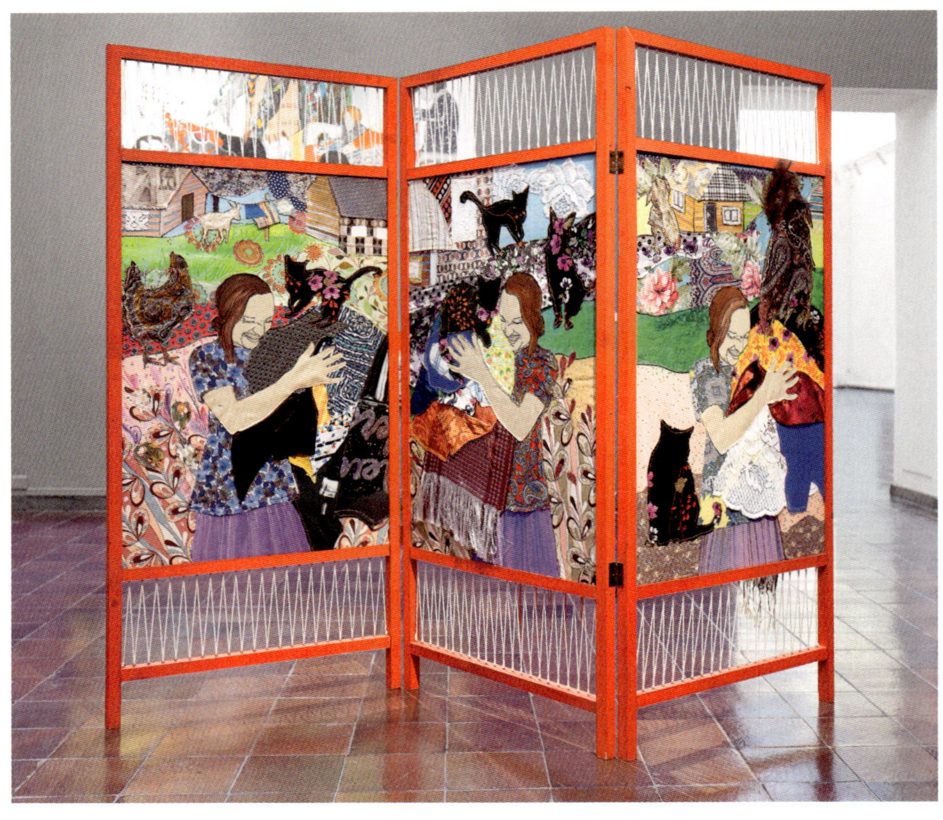

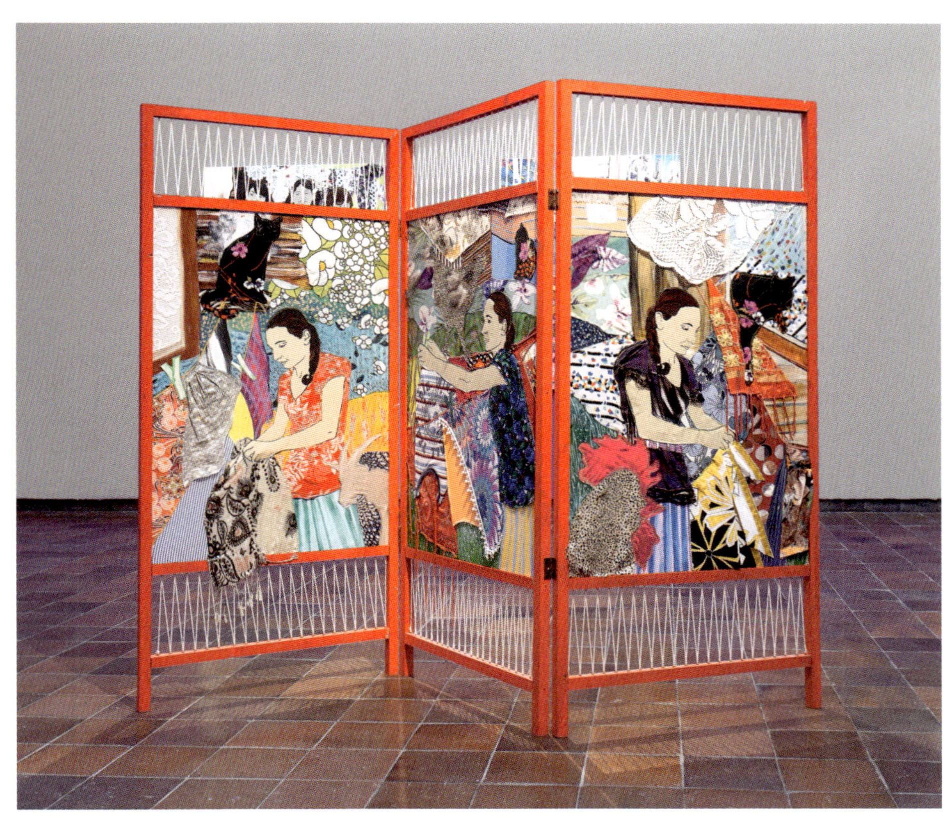

Side Thawenca (Sewn with Threads) 2019
Acrylic paint and fabrics
on wooden screen
155 × 207

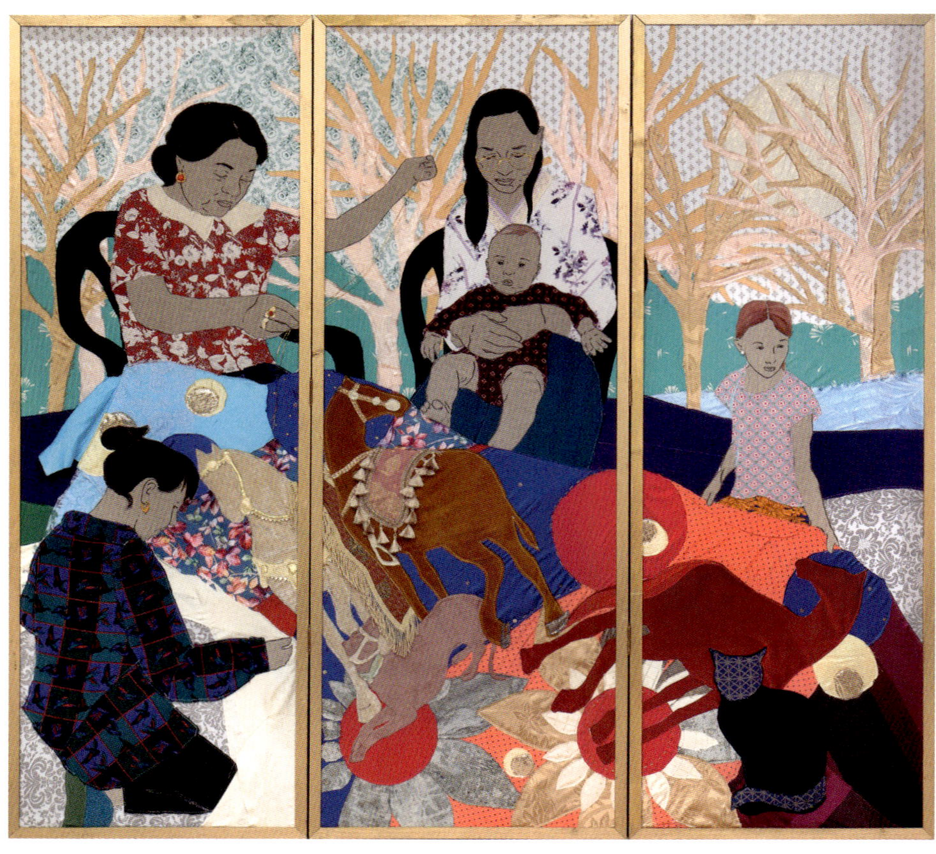

Untitled (After Gentile da Fabriano) 2023
Acrylic paint and fabrics
on wooden screen
3 panels, each: 220 × 76

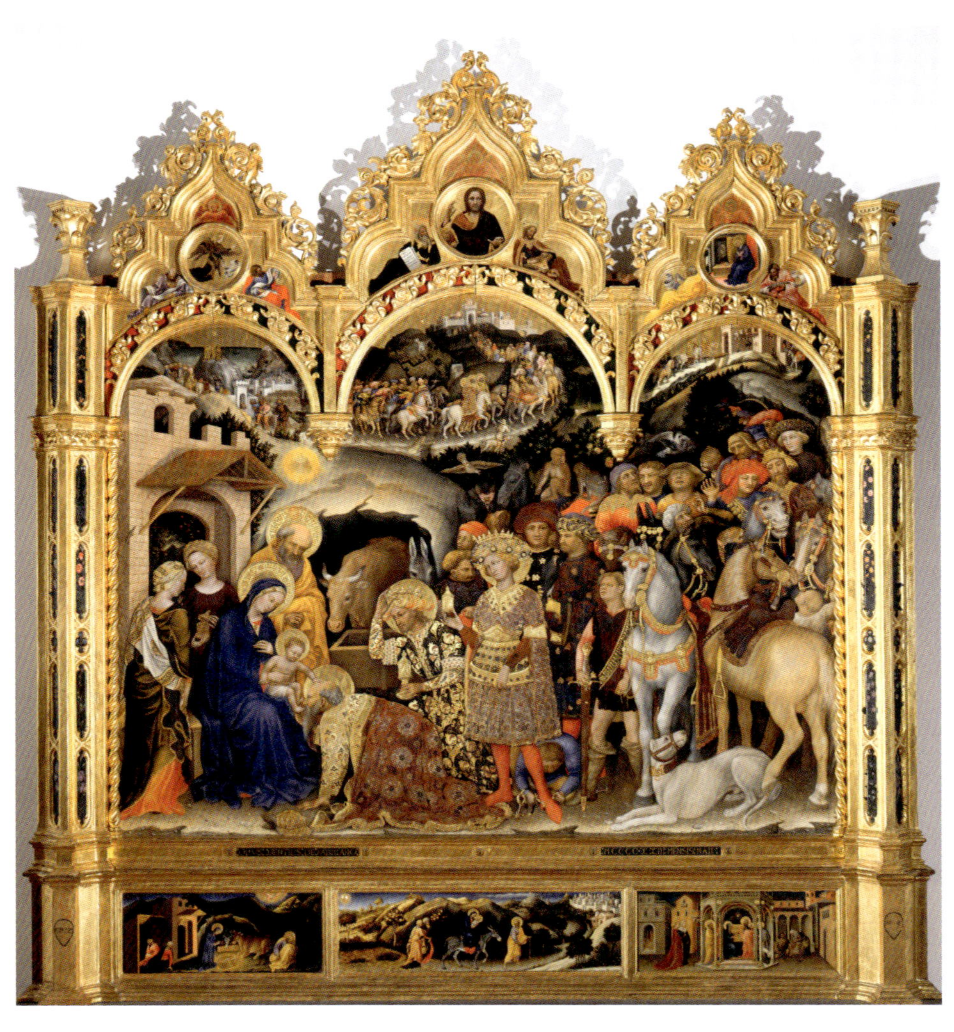

Gentile da Fabriano
Adoration of the Magi 1423
Tempera on wood
300 × 282

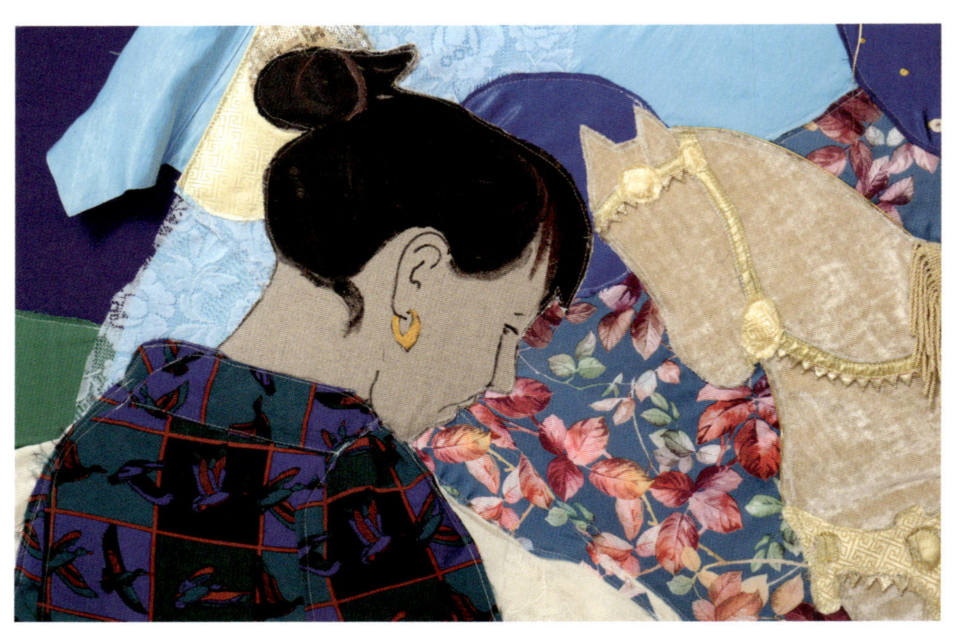

HERE AND OVERLEAF
Details of *Untitled
(After Gentile da Fabriano)* 2023

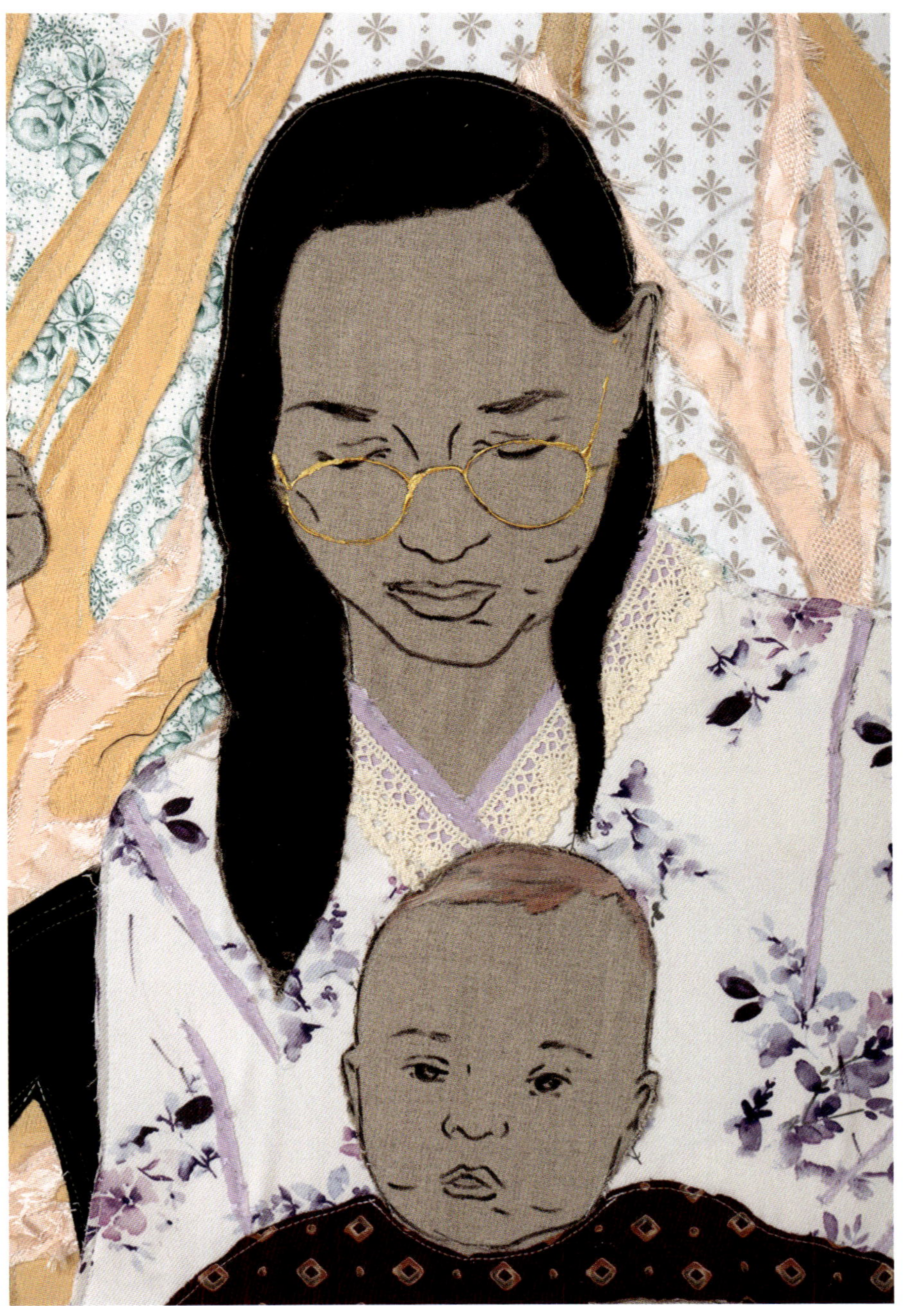

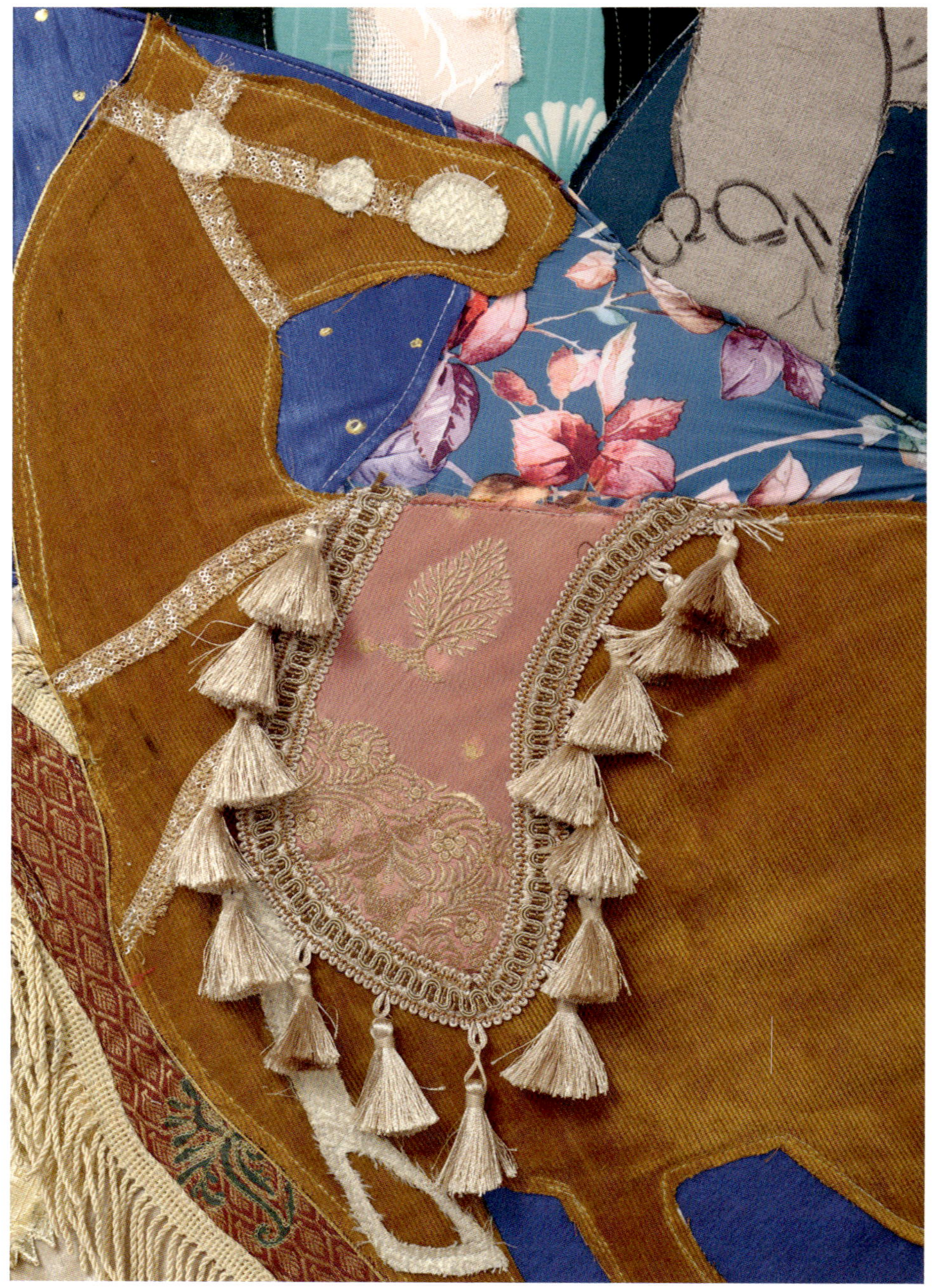

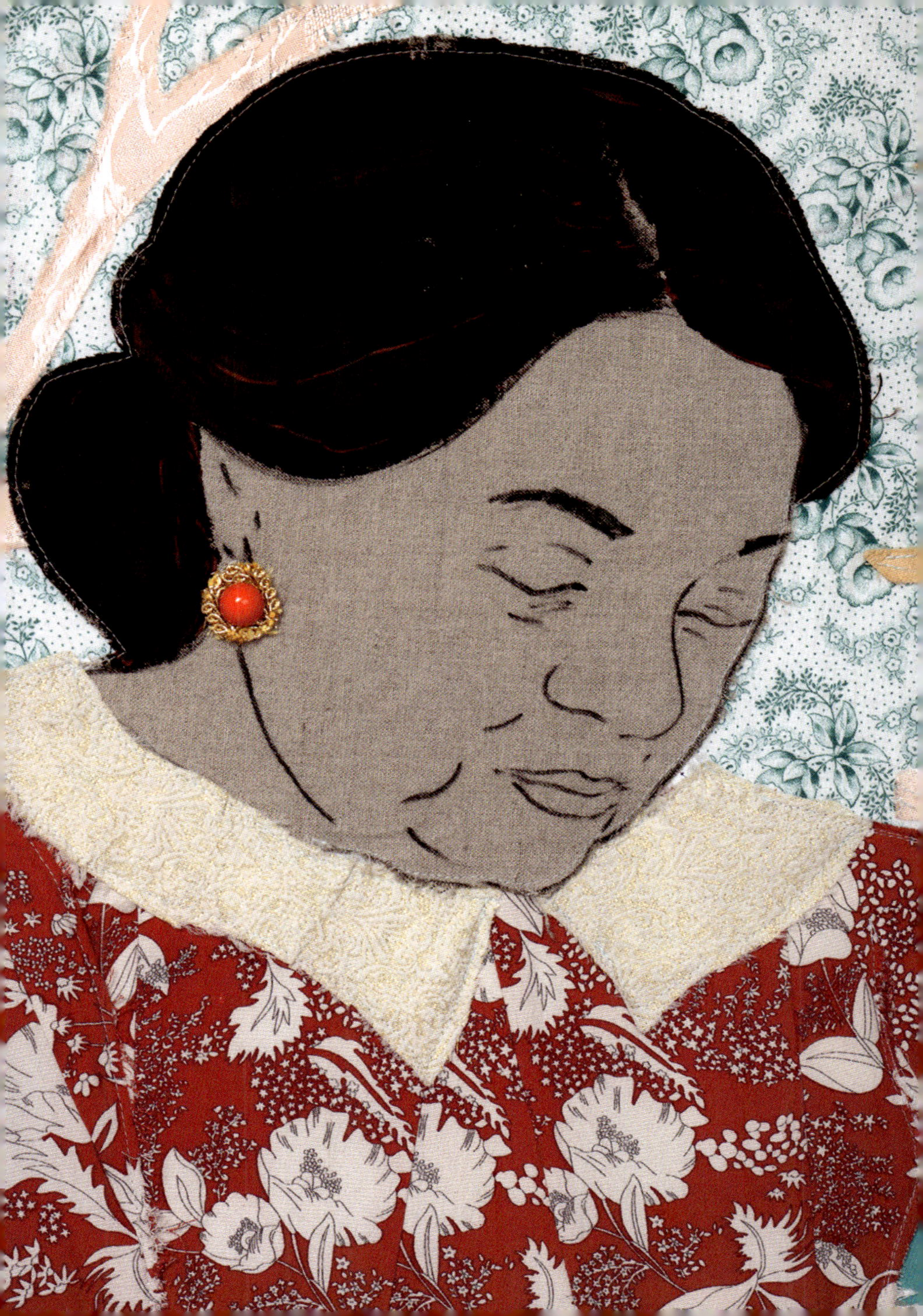

GHOSTS FROM THE MOUNTAINS

Katarzyna
Depta-Garapich

Many non-human beings inhabit Małgorzata Mirga-Tas's works, but the brown bear occupies his own, particularly prominent place. While the colourful, magnificent bears she depicts are related on one hand to the animal's significance in Romani culture, they also serve to materialise the artist's connection with nature and the land by referring to the living bears that inhabit the forest close to her home – the picturesque village of Czarna Góra, which lies at the foot of the Tatra Mountains. Yet the living bear is difficult to encounter, and for many he may be a beast who belongs more to the realm of myths and fairytales than to the natural world. Indeed, in the local highlander tradition, the pronoun 'he' was commonly used to refer to the bear. Substituting the name of the animal with the male pronoun speaks to the animistic and magical

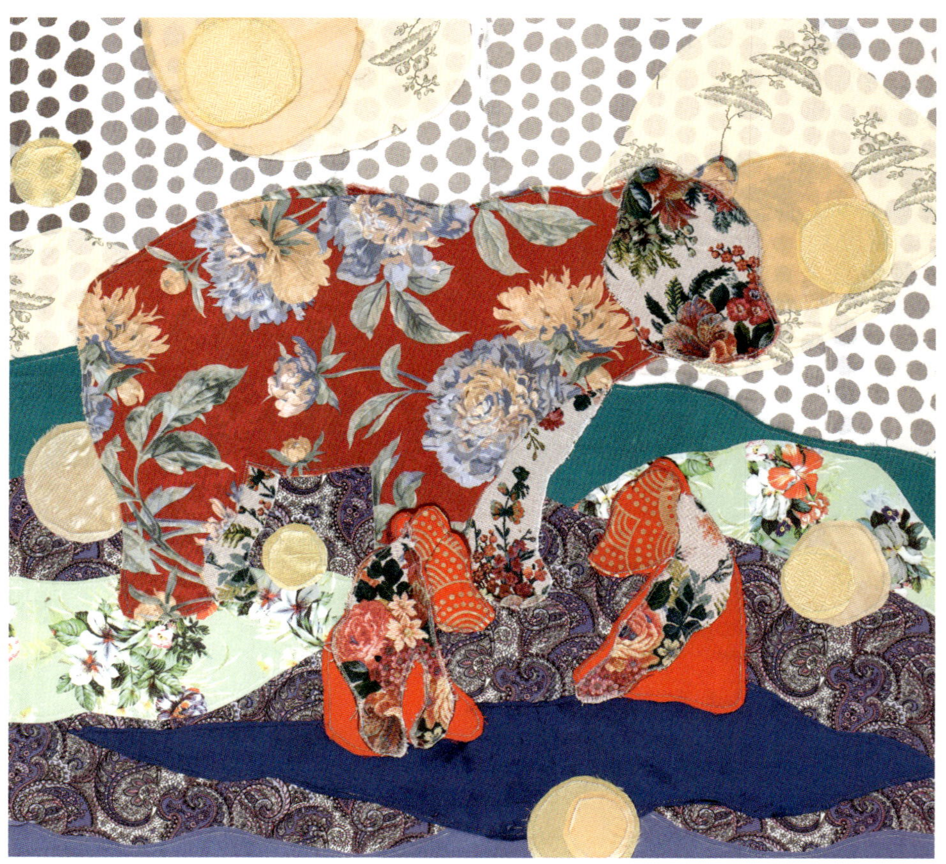

features associated with the bear, which are connected with superstition and with the anthropomorphisation of its image.

The meticulous layering of fabric that constitutes Gosia's textiles resembles the strata of Czarna Góra's mountain landscape. So too do the layers and layers of cardboard, wood or wax from which the artist builds up her sculptural works. Out of this layering emerges a large bear figure, cast in wax mixed with soot. This is not a tame creature; it is a reminder that we are part of a non-human ecosystem that should be treated with respect.

The bear, which represents the relationship between art and nature as well as our interdependence with non-human beings, bonds Gosia's artistic practice with my own. While Gosia's bears keep their conventional shapes intact, my sculptural work is focused on transformation and releasing what is contained within: sharp bear claws emerge from human hands and feet, reminding us of where we come from.

I explored my own connection with the Tatra Mountains in a series titled *Family Album*, a personal work that touches on feelings of loss and belonging. The series consists of drawings over family photographs that were taken by my father during a family trip to the Tatras in the late 1970s. After my parents died, eerie white bears emerged from the photographs in their place, like ghosts. I tried to identify the places my father had photographed – Rzepiska, Bukowina, Białka, Jurgów – although mostly to no avail. But in 2022, as we were installing our exhibition *You ate three hundred devils* at Władysław Hasior Gallery, Tatra Museum in Zakopane, Gosia took one look at the photos and said immediately: 'This is Czarna Góra. That is my aunt's house by the river.'

Familia (Family) 2022
Acrylic paint and fabrics
on canvas
95 × 110

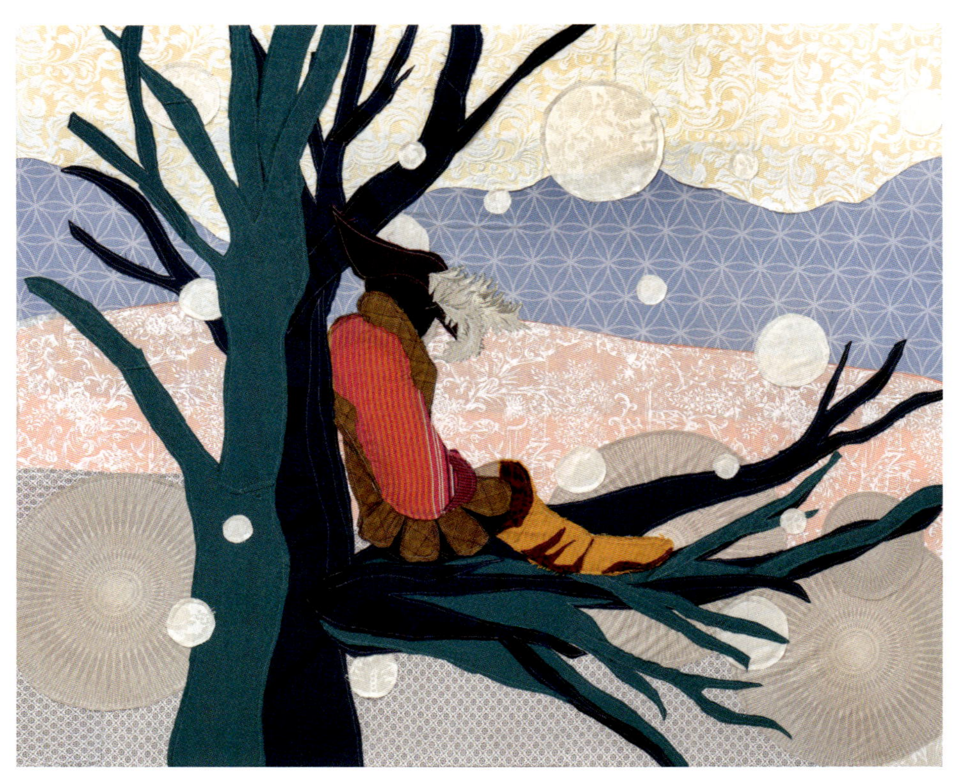

Untitled 2022
Acrylic paint and fabrics
on canvas
137 × 167

BELOW AND OVERLEAF
Roma Pasio Peskro Khier (Roma
in Front of the House) 2024
Acrylic paint and fabrics
on canvas
196 × 196

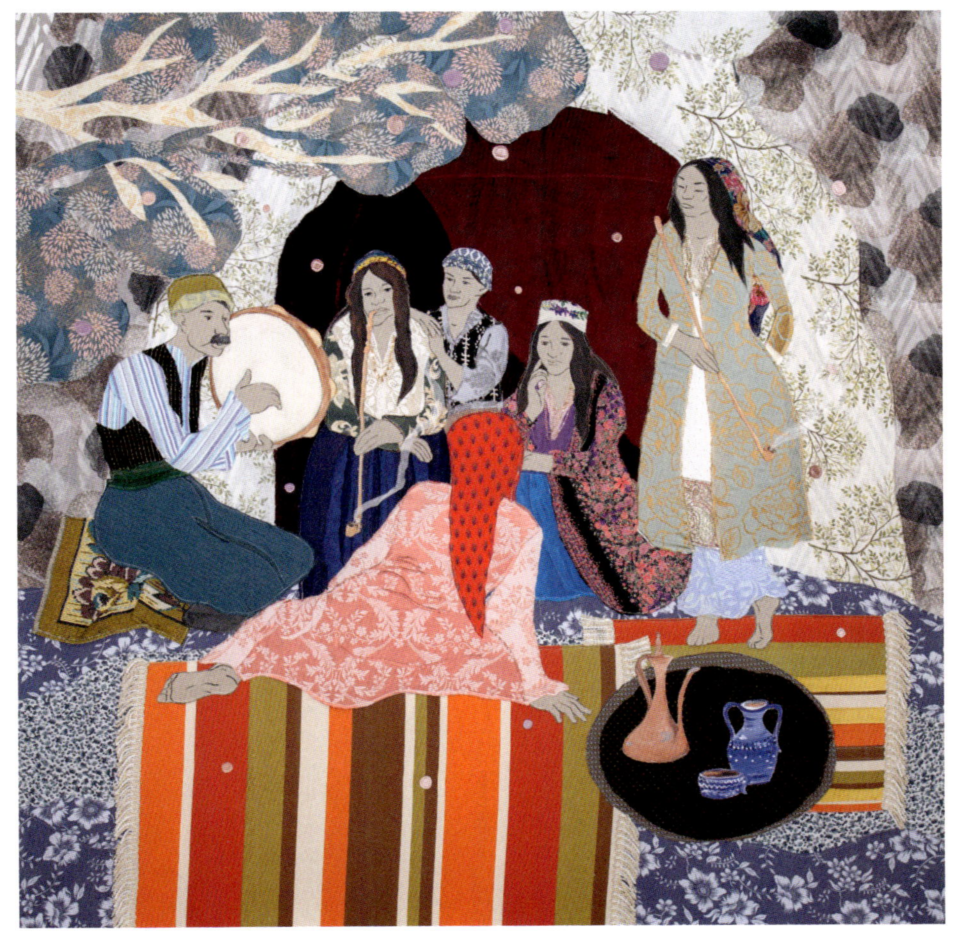

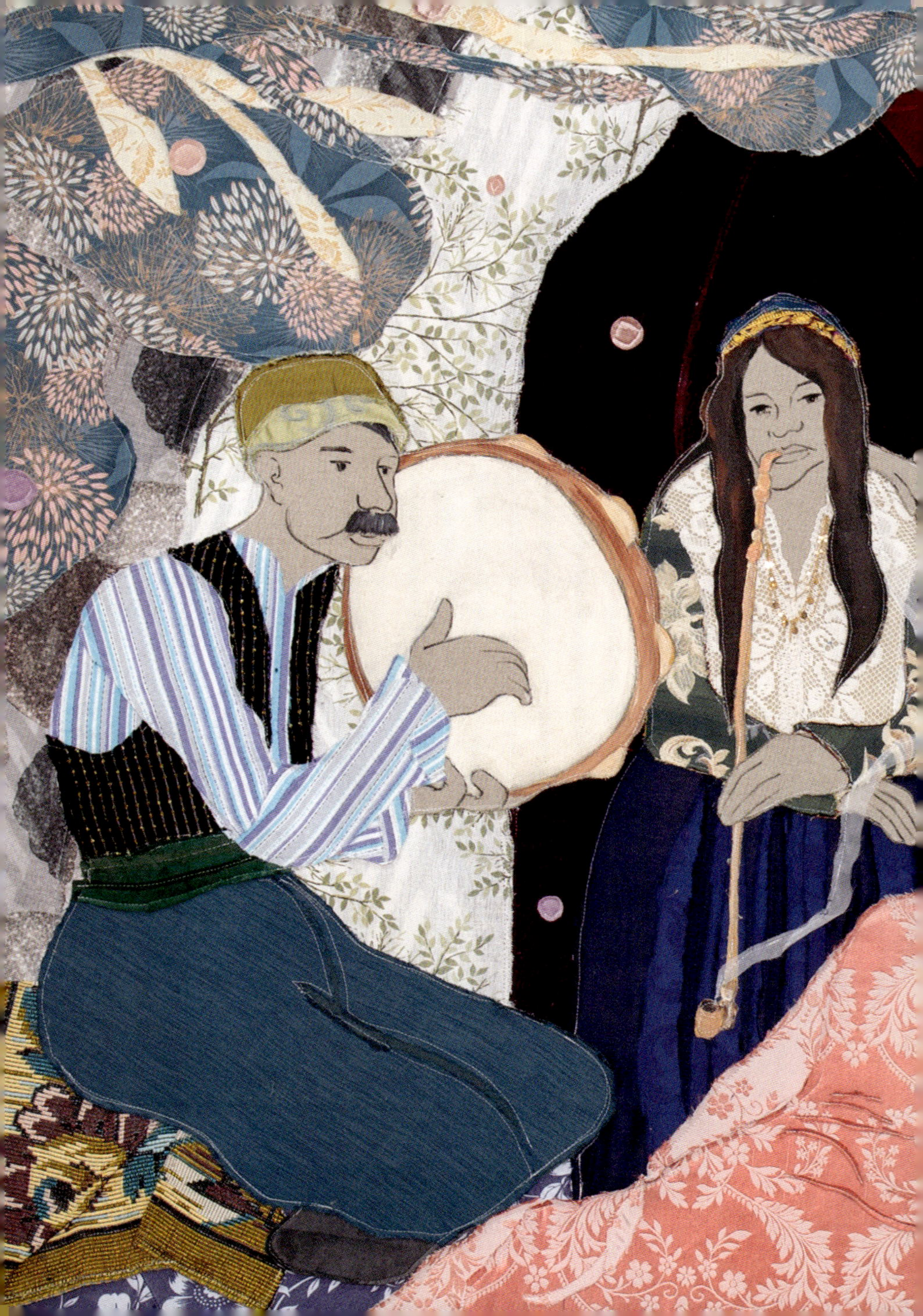

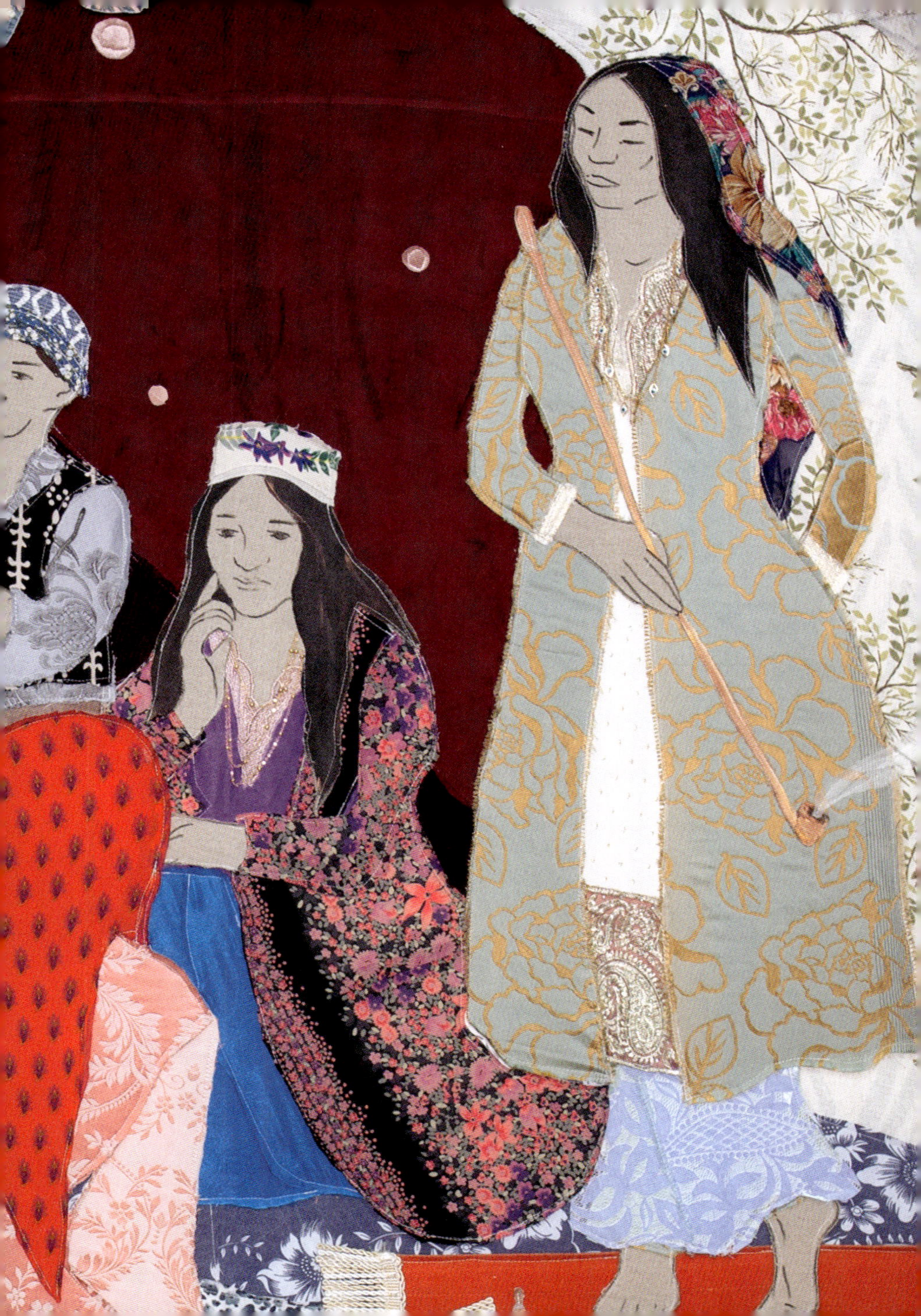

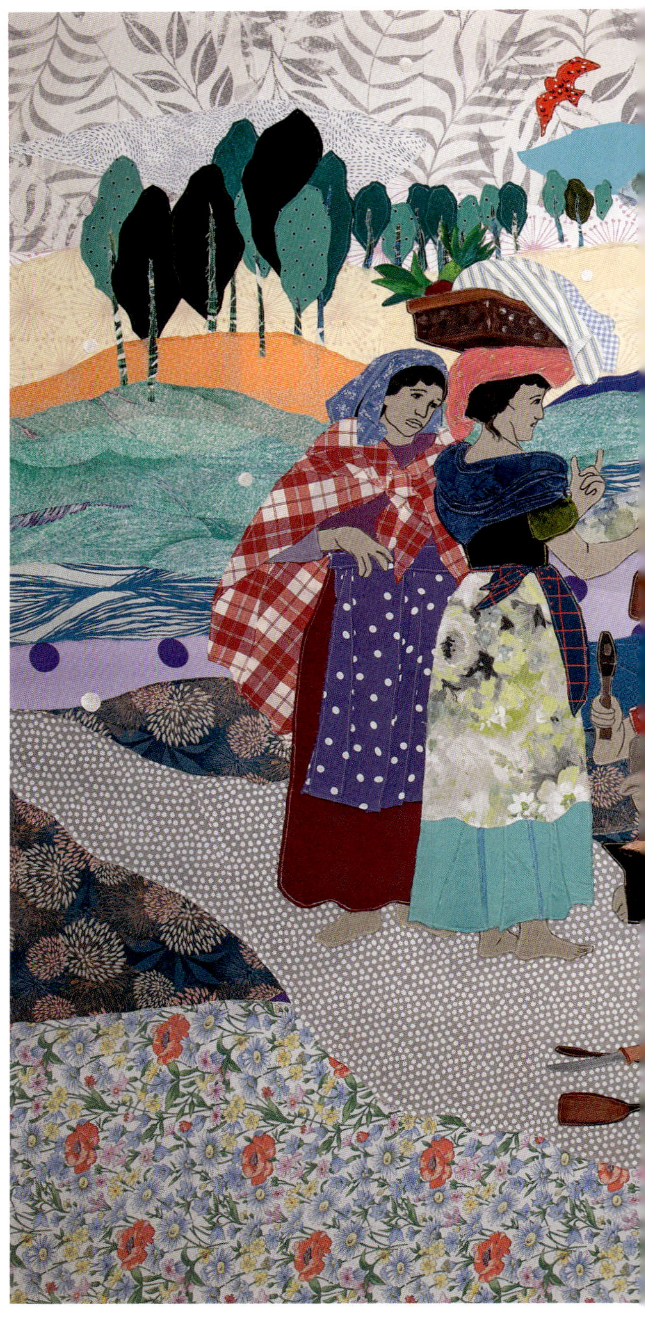

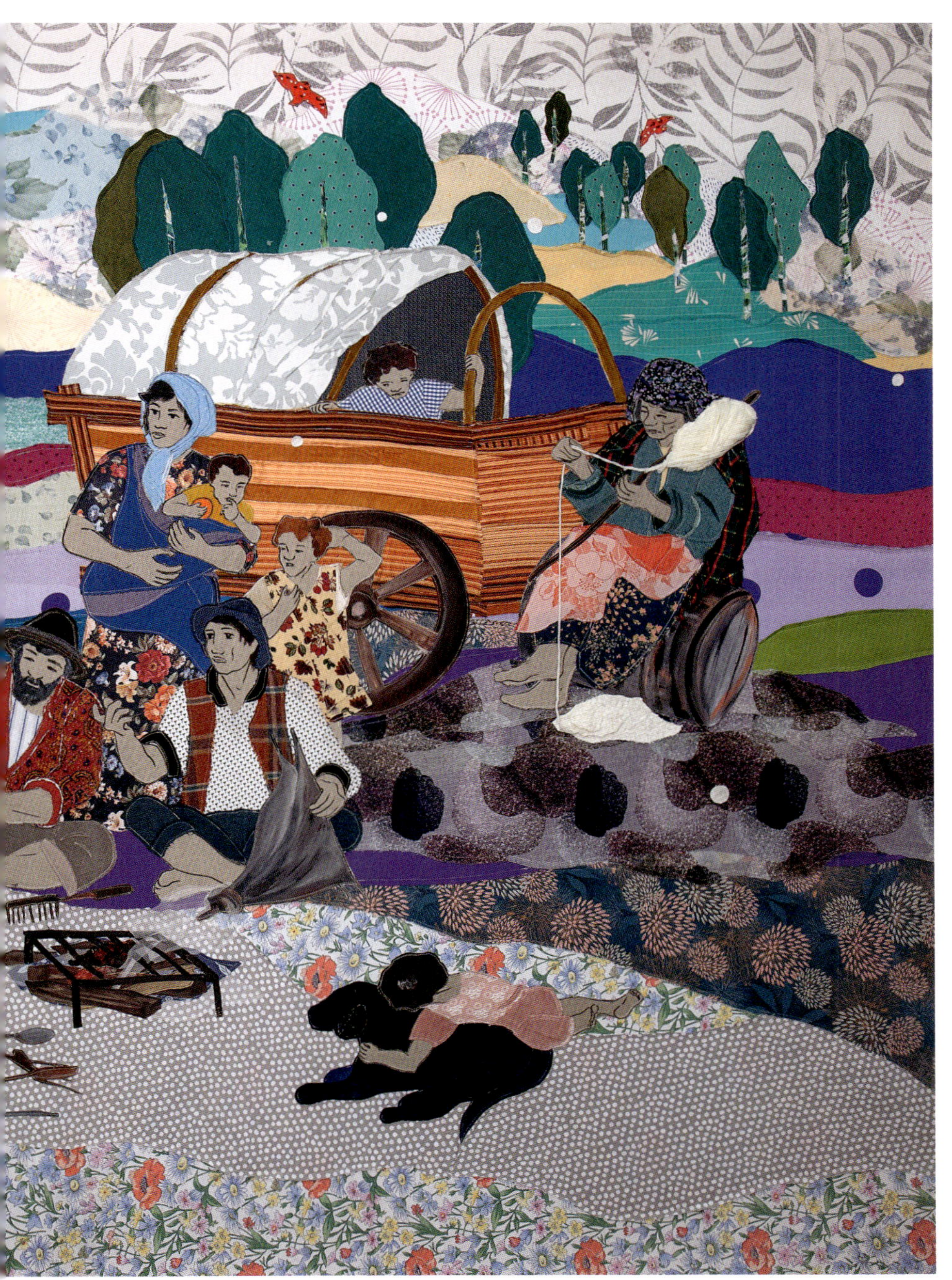

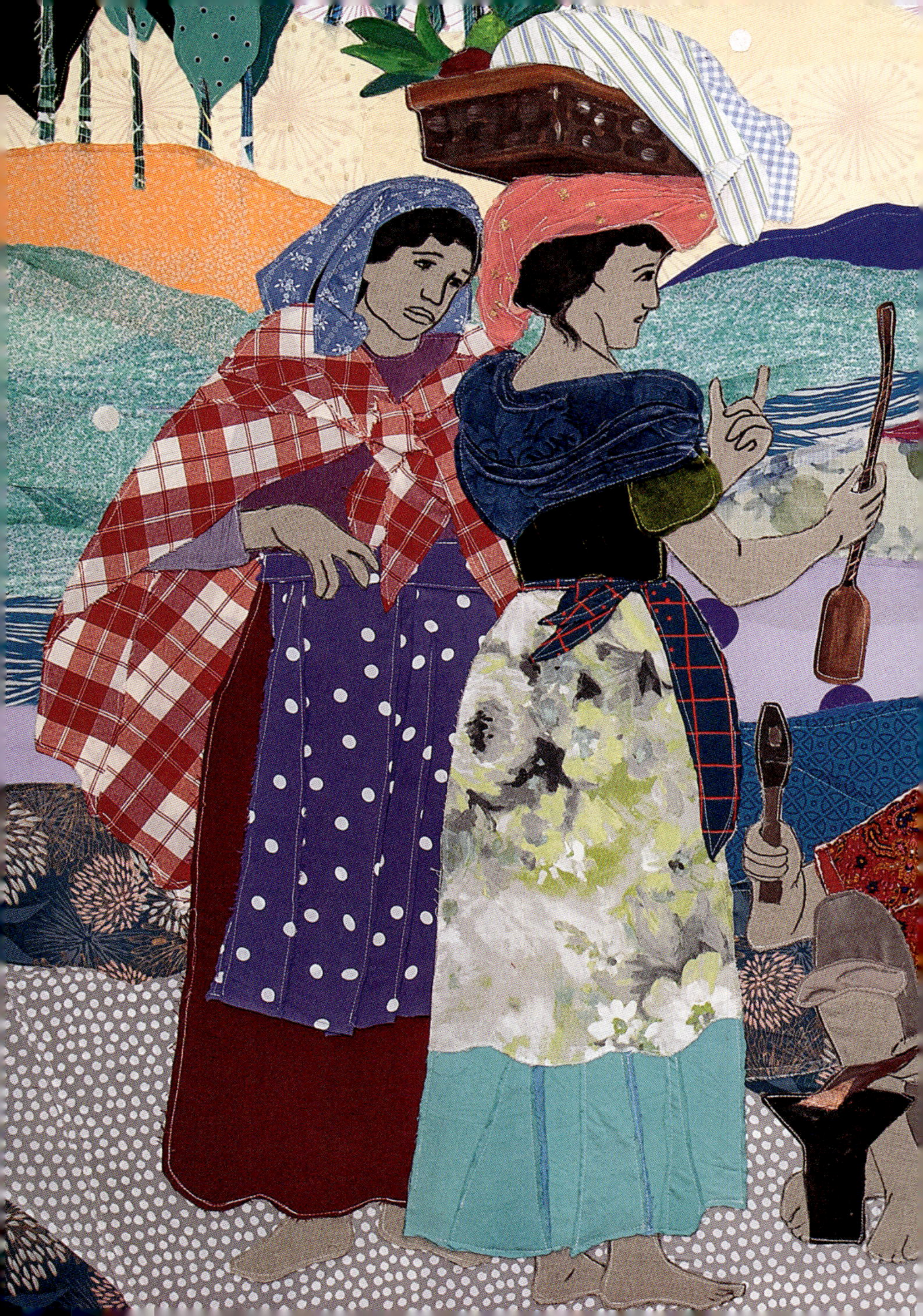

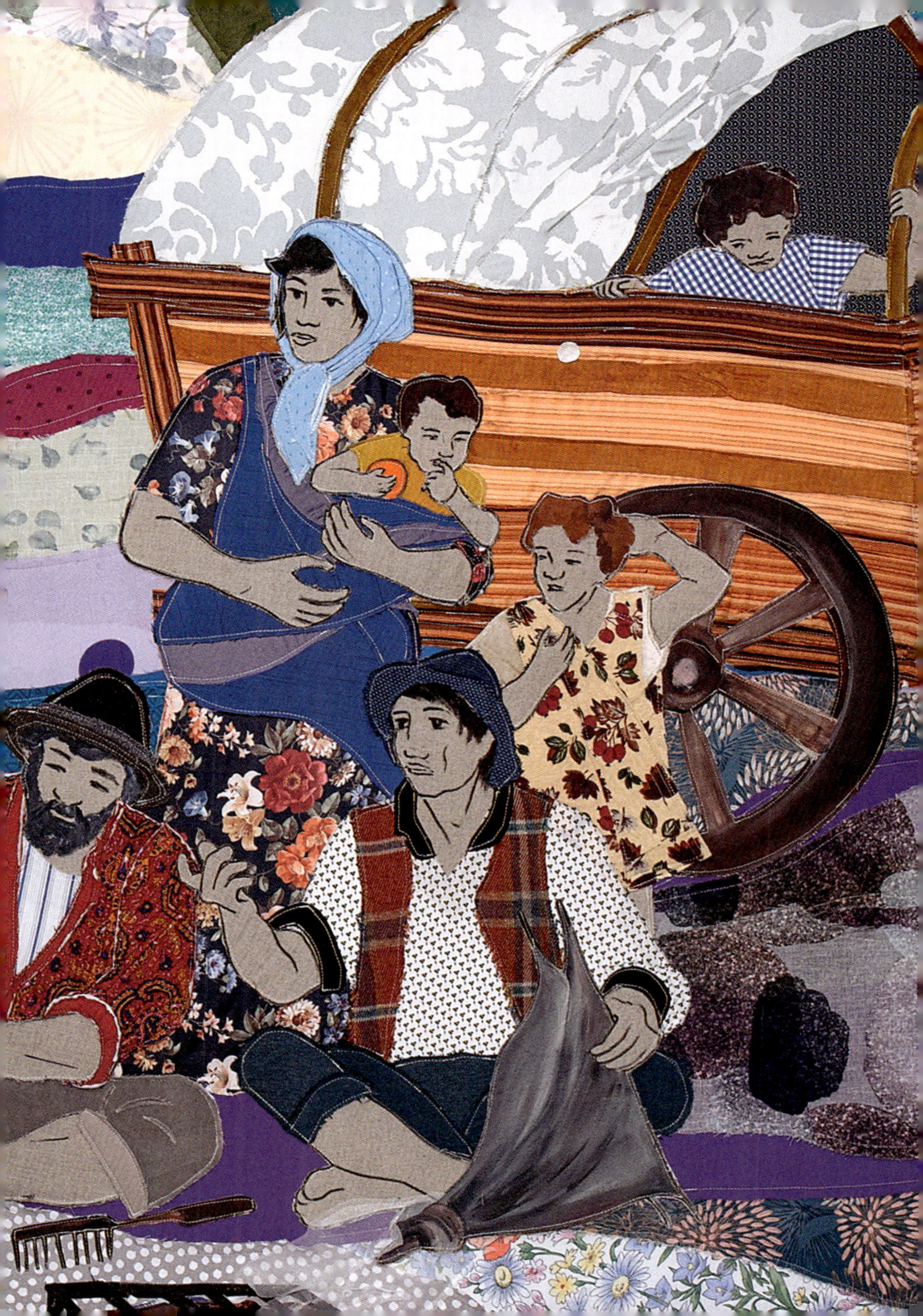

TRAVELLING IMAGES: MAŁGORZATA MIRGA-TAS & JACQUES CALLOT

Wojciech Szymański

In addition to dozens of works by the artist herself, visitors to Małgorzata Mirga-Tas's solo exhibition *Travelling Images* – which opened in December 2022 at the International Cultural Centre in Kraków – could see an installation entitled *Atlas*. The gallery walls were densely filled with more than seventy images of Romani people and artworks representing the Roma, created by non-Romani artists over a period of more than five hundred years – works from various collections, created using disparate techniques and of uneven artistic quality, in which originals loaned for the exhibition hung alongside reproductions of masterpieces from famous European collections.

The installation's scope was the history of the visual colonisation of the Roma by hegemonic European culture. By exhibiting together various artworks that had the Roma people and their culture as their subject, it showed the violence of European artistic practice in creating the racialised subject and its long persistence. Moreover, among the works shown in the *Atlas* were several that have served Mirga-Tas as critical points of reference, of re-appropriation, of inspiration – to reclaim the histories of the Roma and their representations, and also to question the hegemony of the white gaze. In her work Mirga-Tas often returns to the history of European art; as a Romani person herself, belonging to the transnational, cross-border subgroup of Bergitka, and therefore a member of one of the ethnic groups still most discriminated against in Europe, she is fully aware of the role that art has played in the formation of racial prejudices and racist stereotypes.

Mirga-Tas's *Atlas* included four etchings by the Lorraine painter Jacques Callot entitled *The Gypsies* 1621–31 (pp.44–5), also known as *Life of the Egyptians*; like many Europeans of his age, Callot believed that the Roma originated in Egypt. These masterpieces of early modern engraving are among the most significant images of the Roma in the history of European art. Callot depicted caravans of dangerous armed wanderers from the East, wearing spectacular costumes and feathered hats, travelling on horseback and on foot, dragging their belongings in chariots. We observe, too, the stereotypical images of Romani life, in movement and at rest: vagrancy, stealing, fortune telling, bivouacking, meals prepared in cauldrons hung over the fire. It is an existence depicted as difficult and precarious, but not without picturesque aspects. Undoubtedly, the engravings are to be interpreted in the context of the

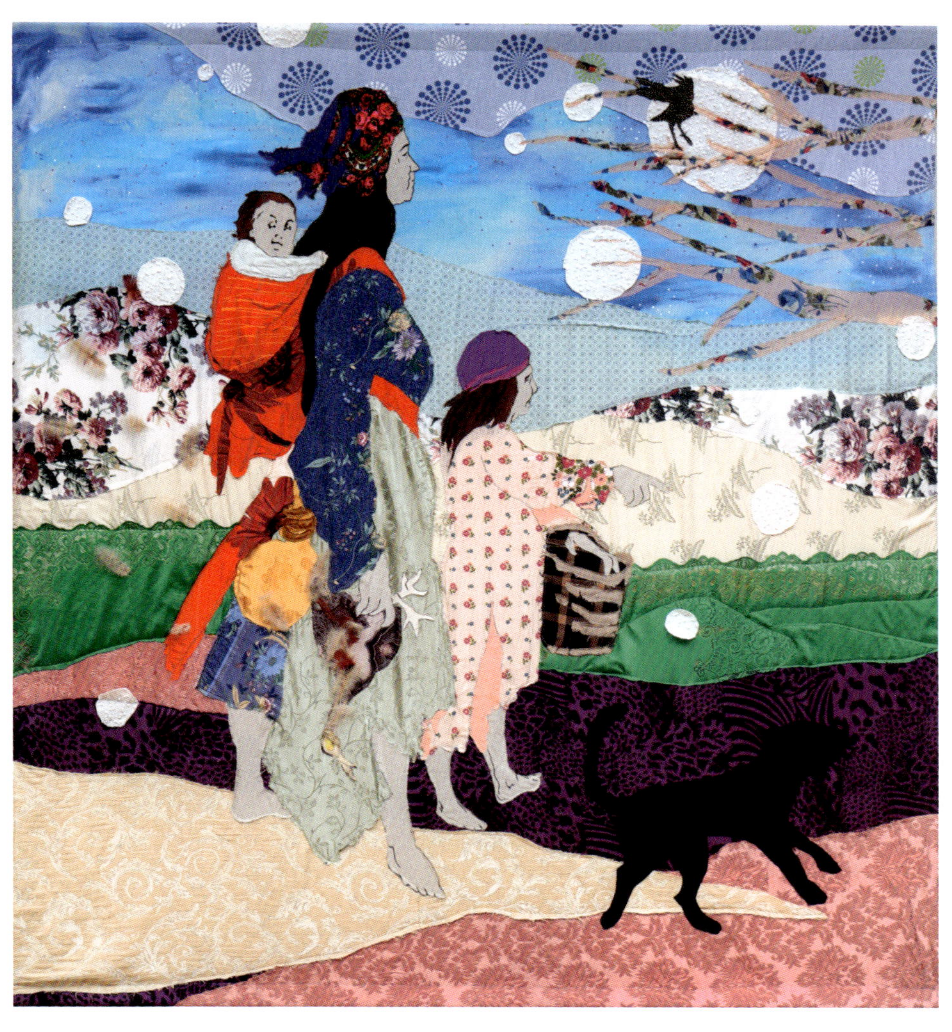

Out of Egypt from the
series *Out of Egypt* 2021
Acrylic paint and fabrics
on canvas
231 × 208

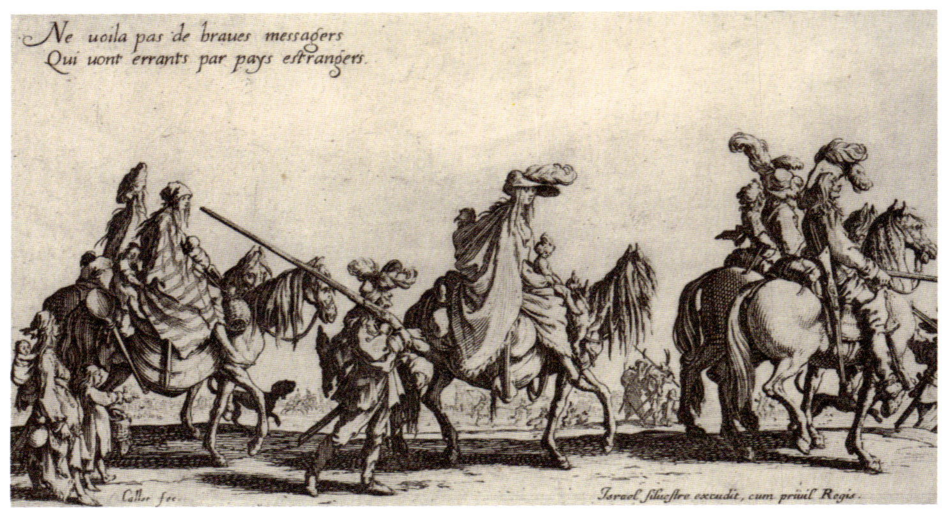

Jacques Callot
The Marching Gypsies: The Advance Guard from the series *The Gypsies* 1621–31
Etching on paper
12.5 × 23.6

Jacques Callot
The Stopping Place of the Gypsies: The Fortune-Tellers from the series *The Gypsies* 1621–31
Etching on paper
12.5 × 23.6

French couplets that accompanied them: sarcastic and full of prejudice, these lines are unequivocal testimony to the negative attitude of settled Europeans of the time towards the nomadic people then called Gypsies.

Mirga-Tas reworked Callot's engravings to create an exquisite series of large-format textiles entitled *Out of Egypt* 2021 (p.43). As she could draw on neither any (non-existent) Romani self-representations of the time nor any historical evidence of how the Roma perceived themselves, she decided to perform a gesture of artistic reappropriation, choosing some parts of Callot's original compositions and omitting others that she considered inappropriate. By eliminating the texts that originally accompanied the engravings, Mirga-Tas literally erased their stigmatising and derisive message. By changing their scale and creating her images using another technique, reminiscent of the fine tapestries of the seventeenth century, she altered not just the size of the images but the stature of the figures in them. By using various multicoloured and tactile materials, she reanimated the characters from Callot's engravings, giving them new life. Mirga-Tas's reappropriation thus simultaneously involves a restitution of history and the reclaiming of control over wandering images: historical and contemporary methods of creating a visual narrative of the Roma people. The series was created for a solo show at the Arsenał Gallery in Białystok in 2021 and made available to the

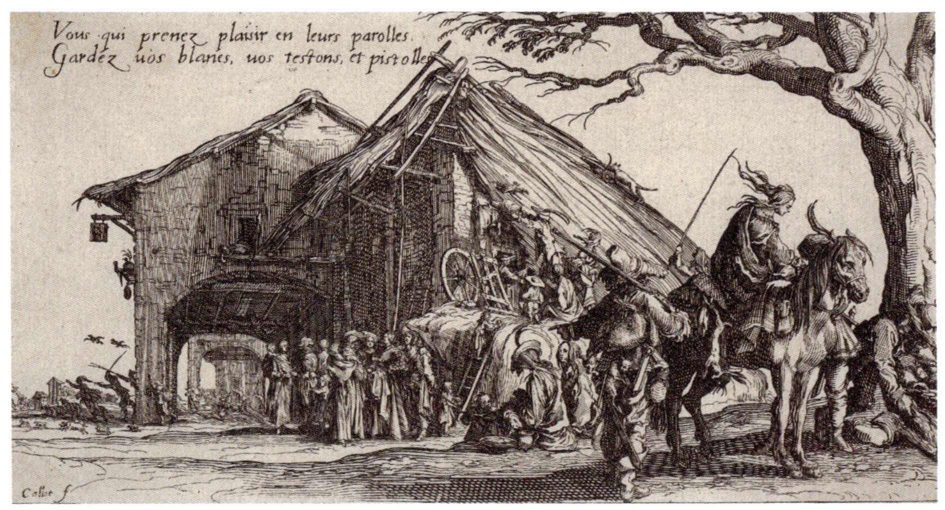

OVERLEAF
Małgorzata Mirga-Tas
Details from the panels
January (above) and *August*
(below) from *Re-enchanting
the World* 2022
Acrylic paint and fabrics
on canvas
462 × 498 × 7 and 462 ×
541 × 7

international public a year later at Documenta XV in Kassel. However, this was not Mirga-Tas's last encounter with the Lorraine engraver. For her solo exhibition *Re-enchanting the World* in the Polish Pavilion of the 2022 Venice Biennale, the artist again drew on Jacques Callot's engravings, using them as the basis for a frieze depicting a colourful caravan, the mythical journey of the Roma from the East to Europe (pp.46–7). This exhibition at Tate St Ives is another stopping place on the journey of these travelling images.

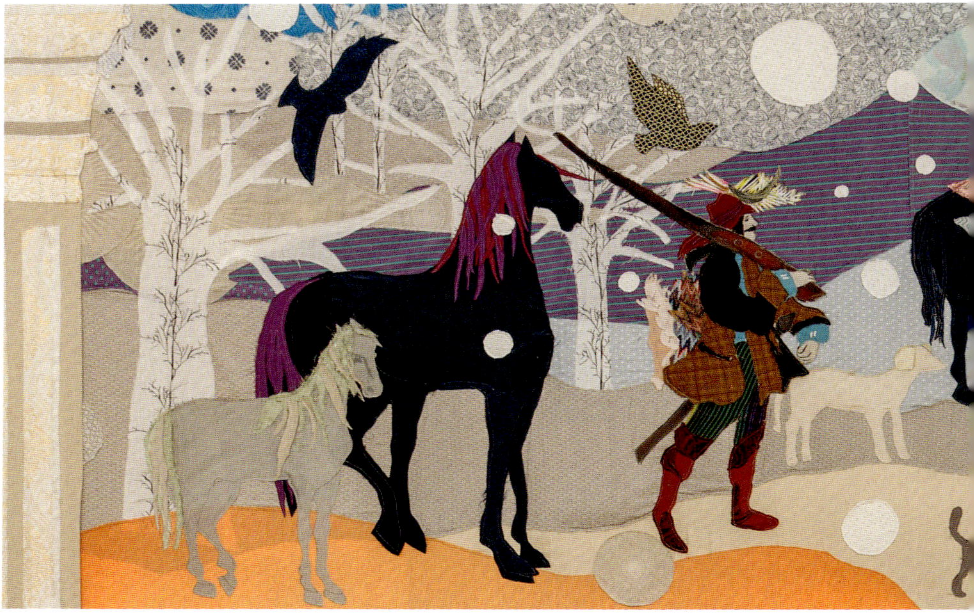

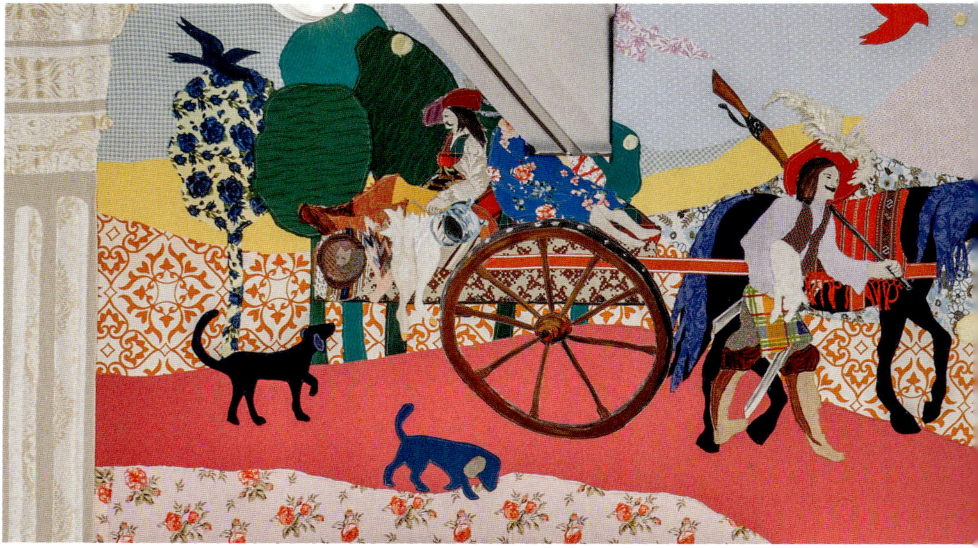

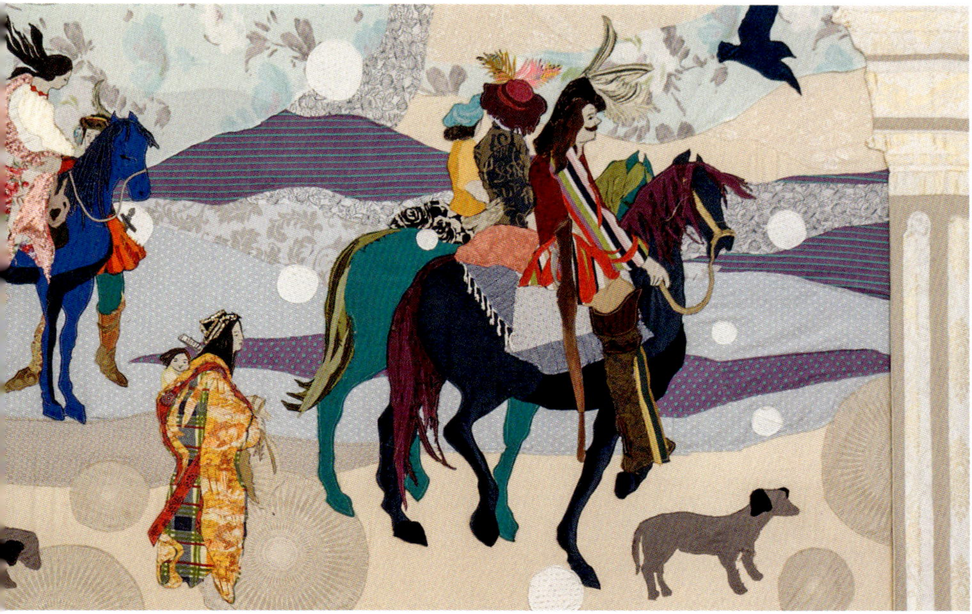

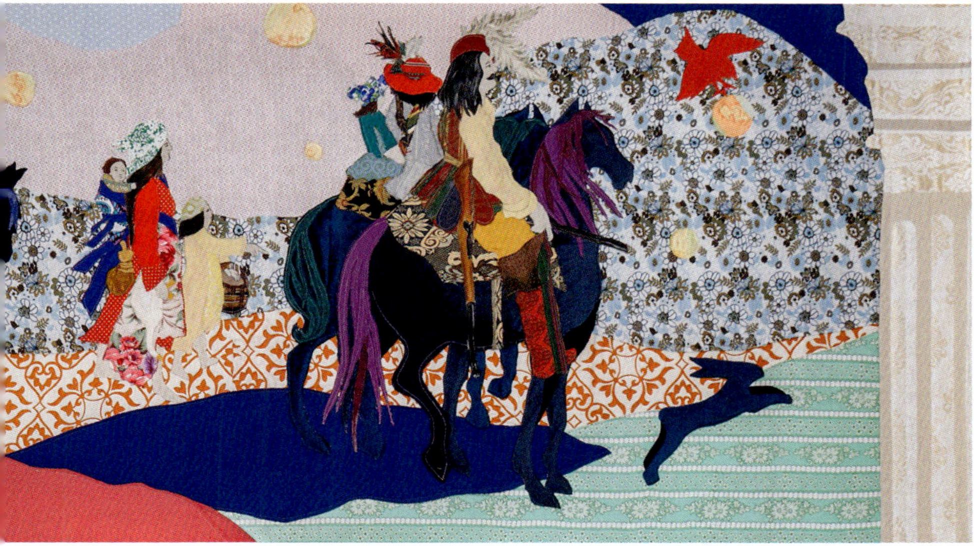

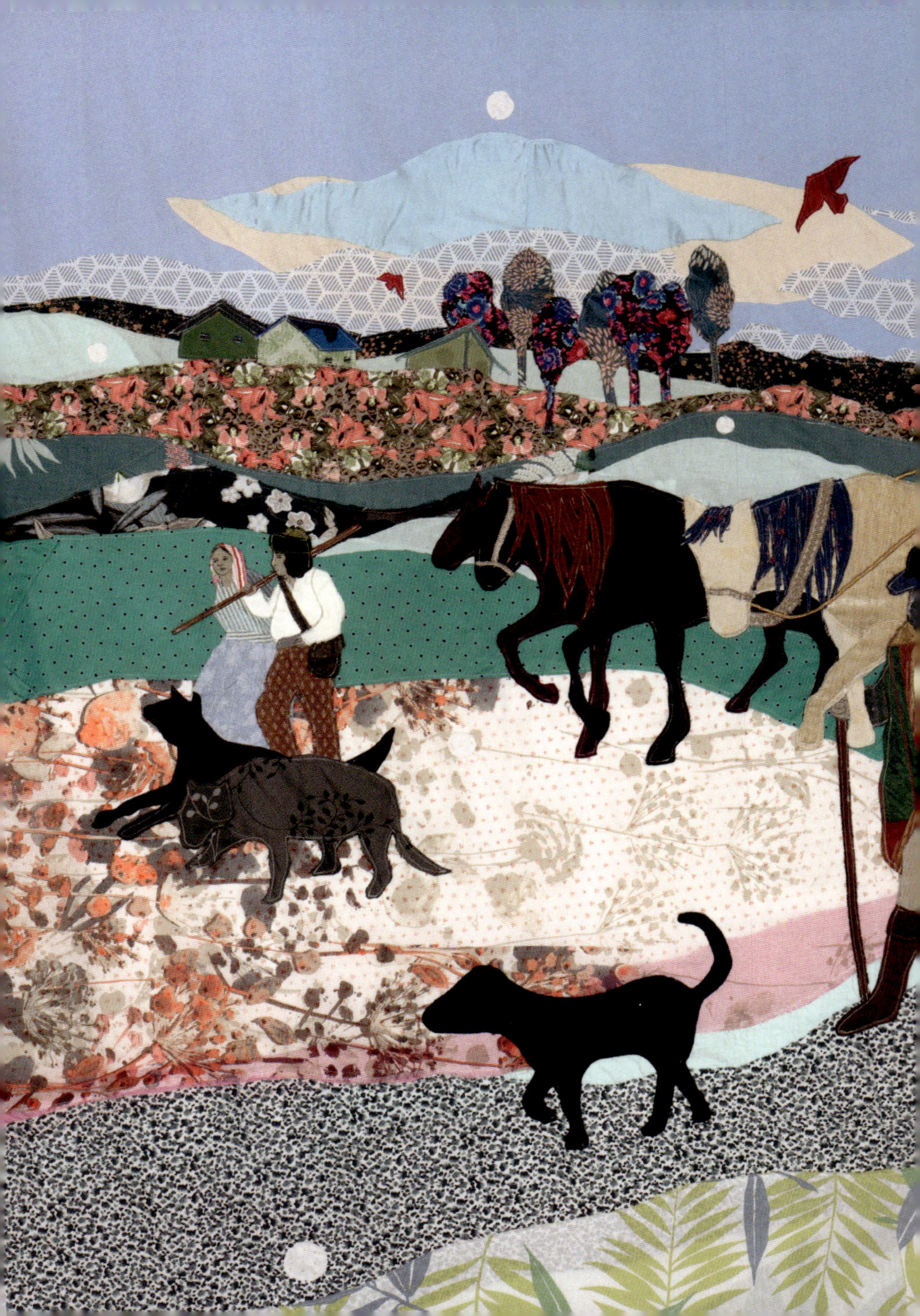

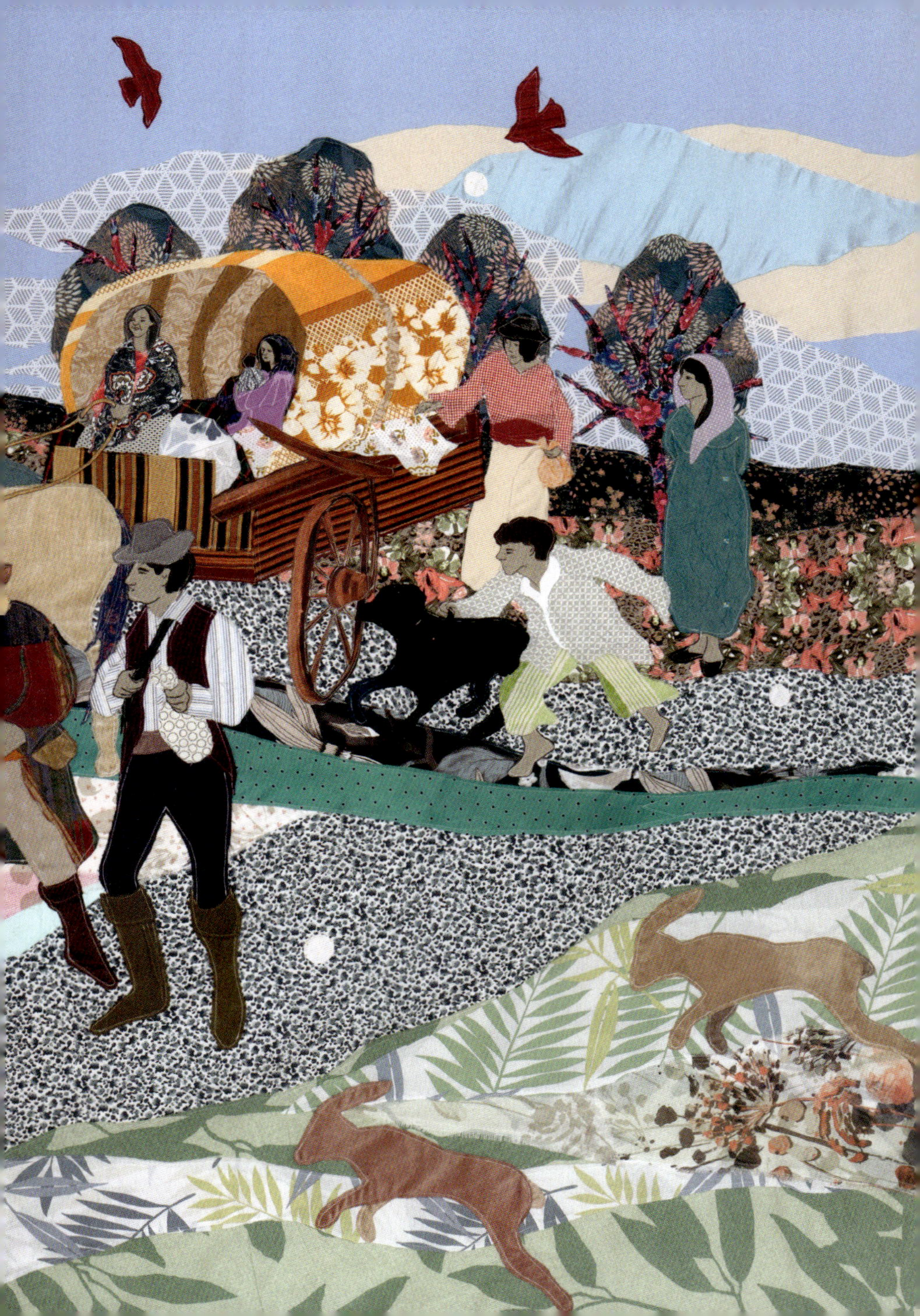

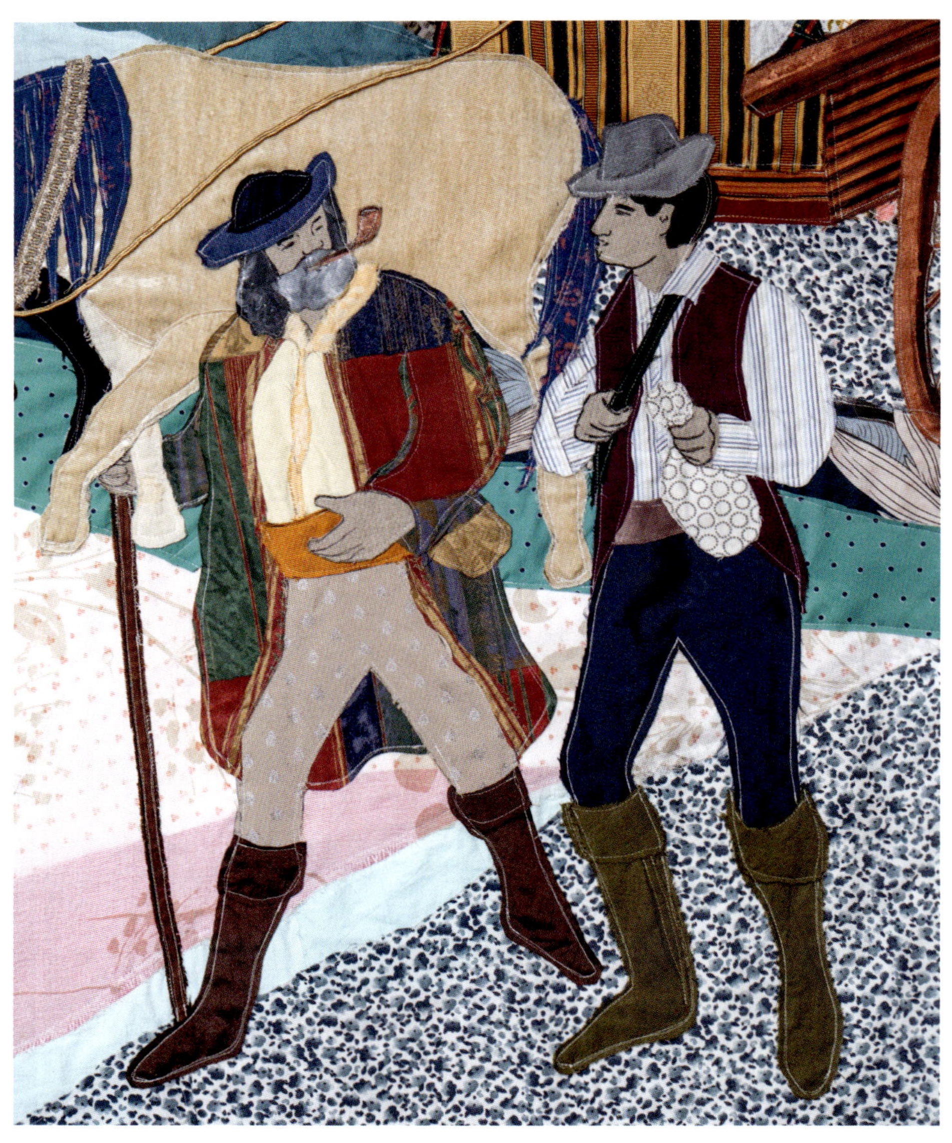

Dromeskri zuta (On the Journey) 2024
Acrylic paint and fabrics on
canvas
228.5 × 313

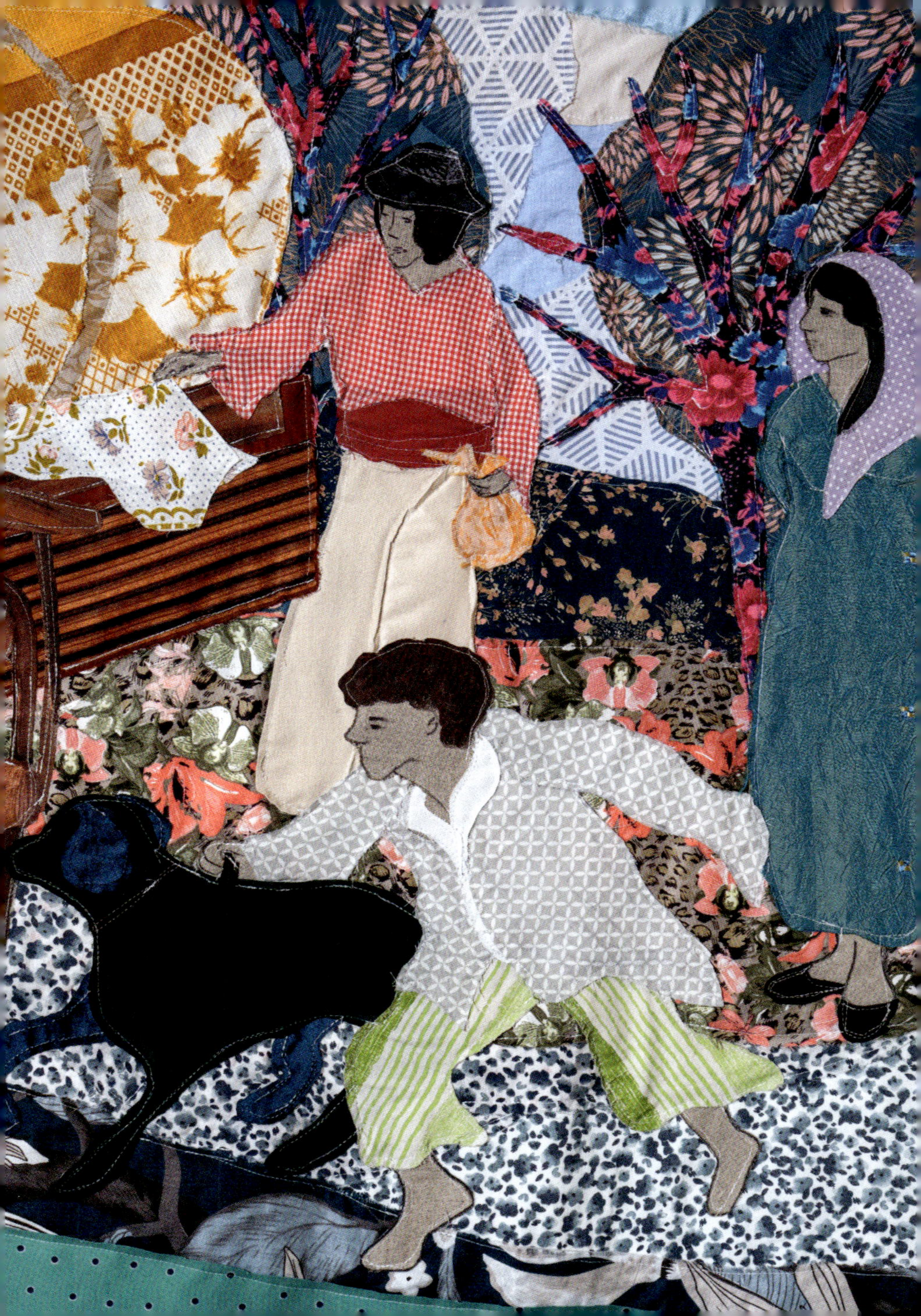

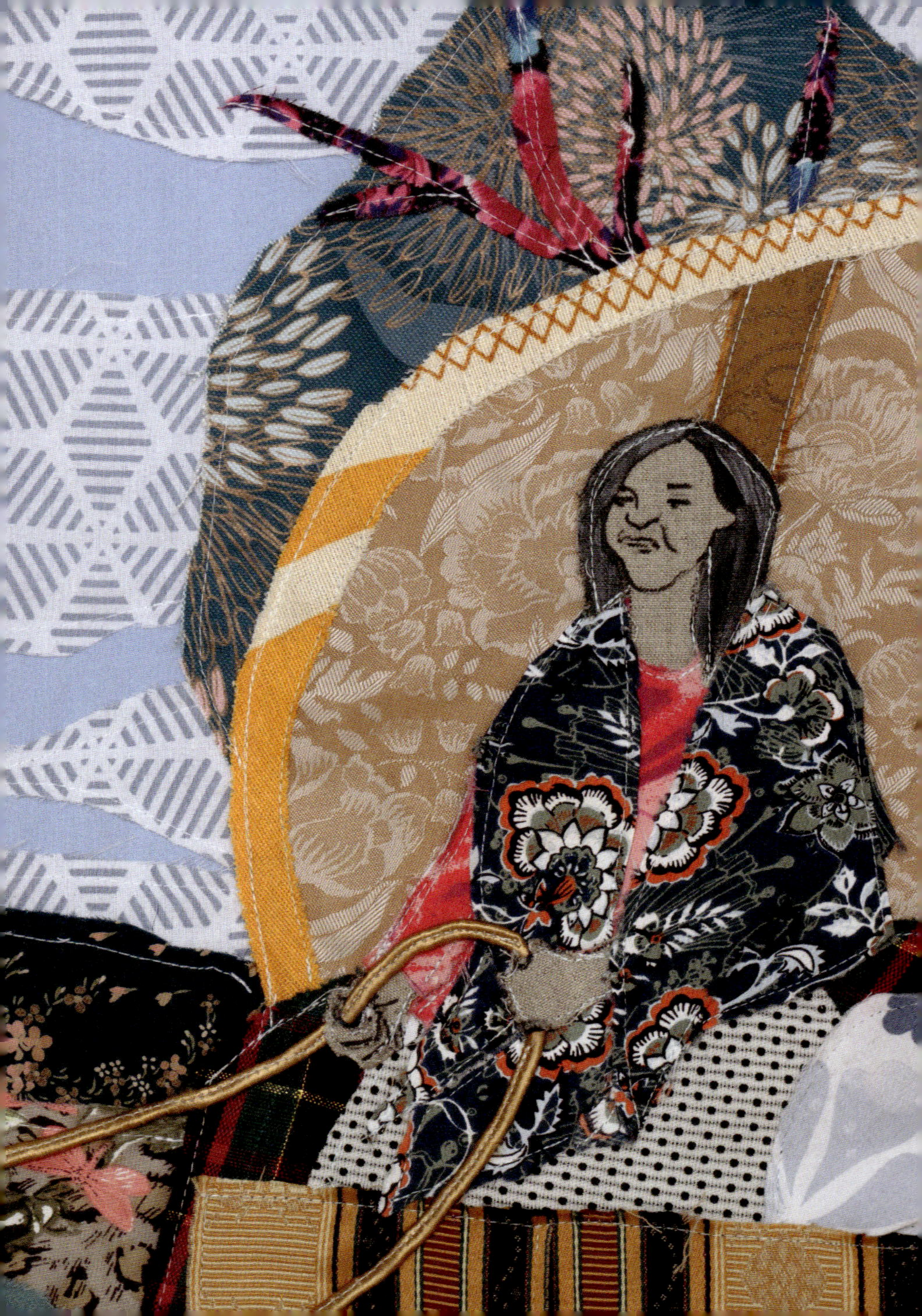

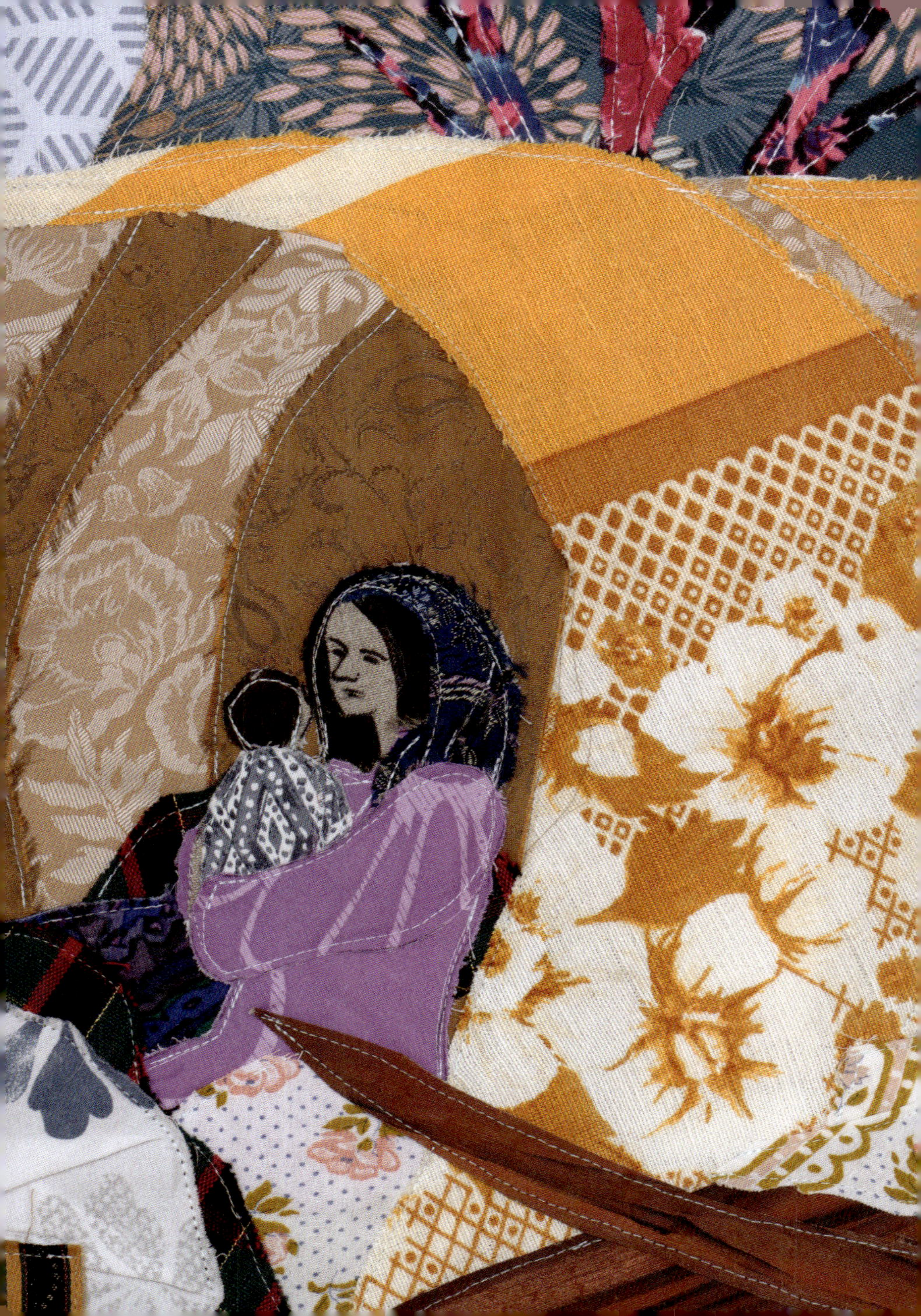

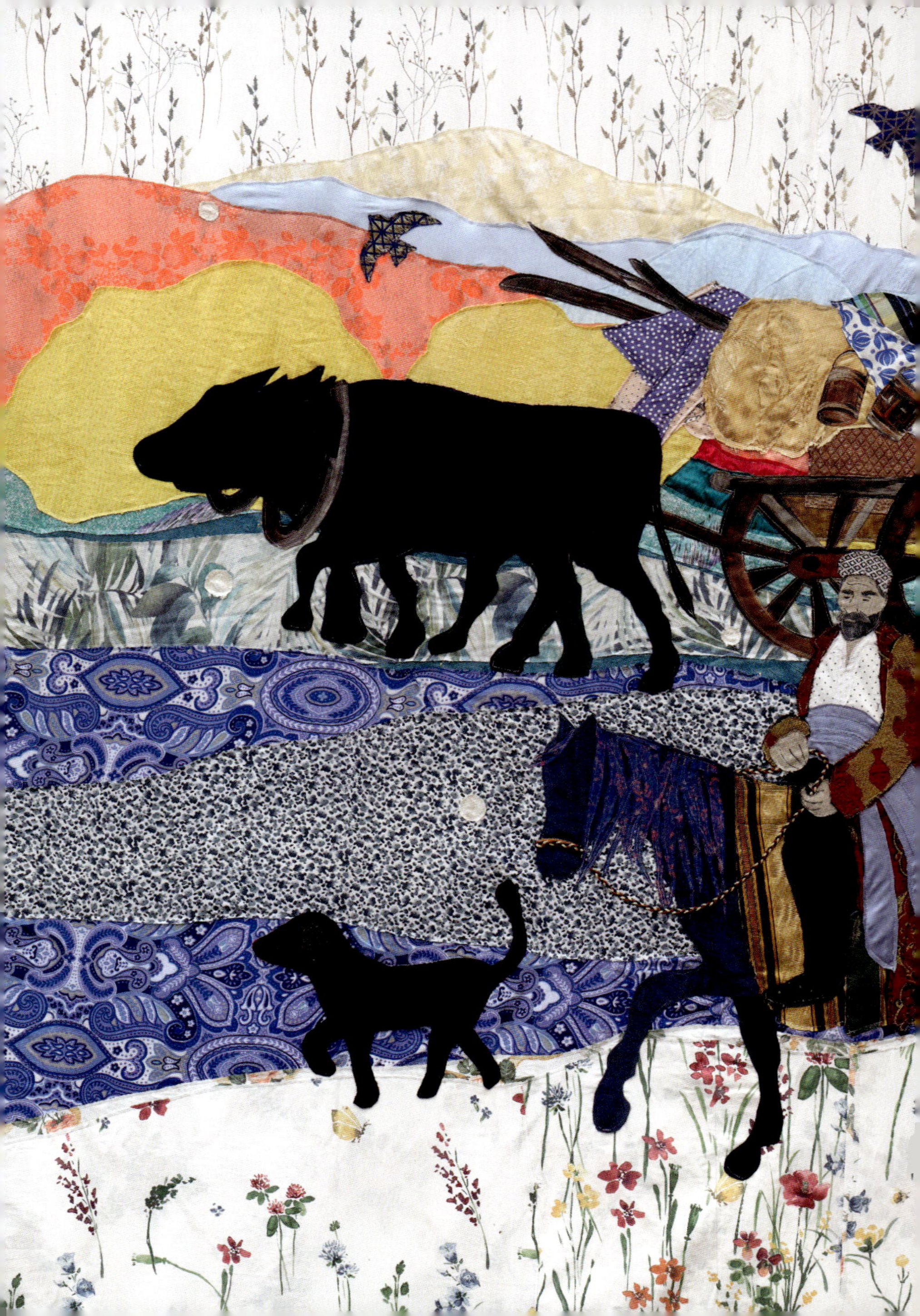

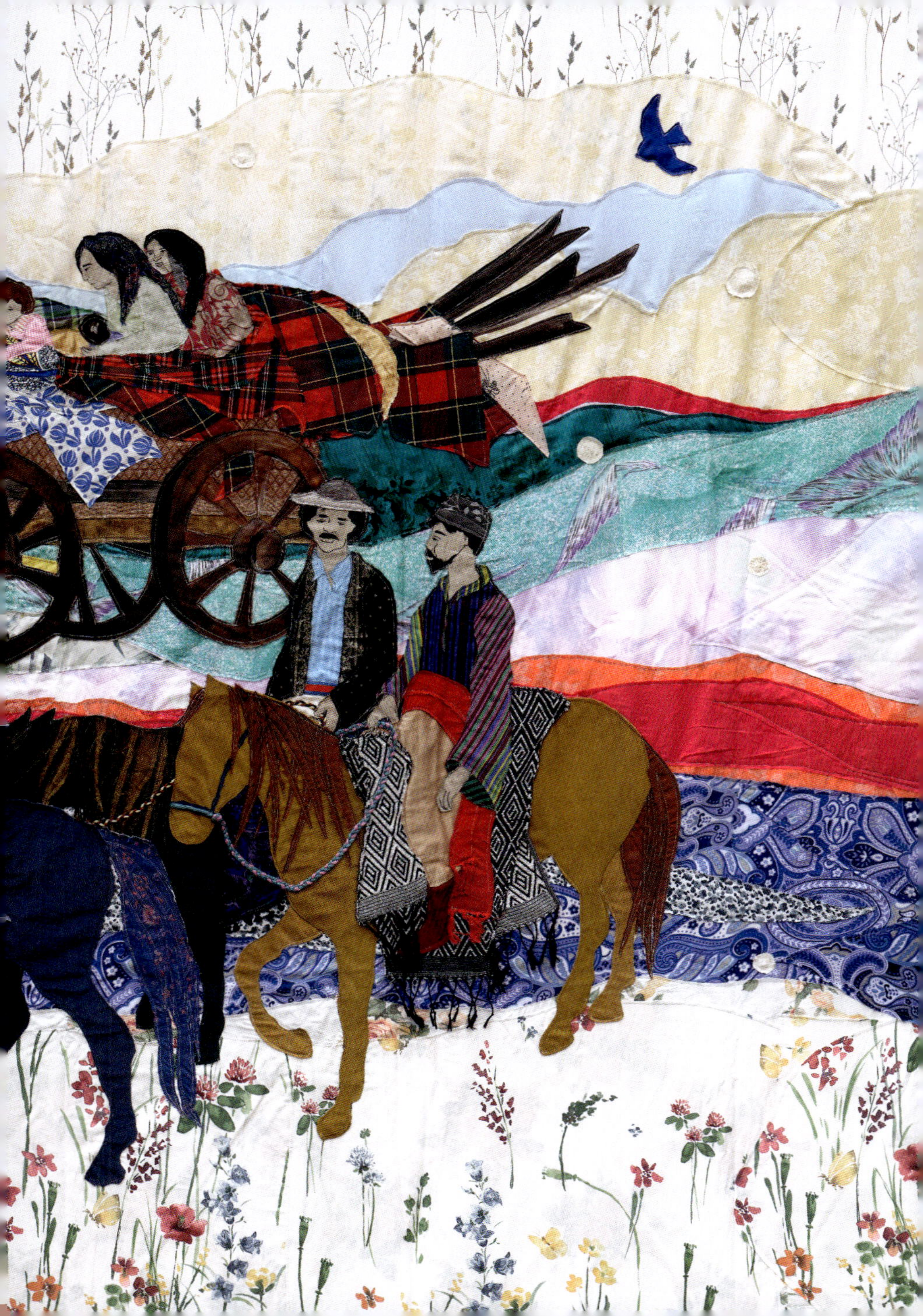

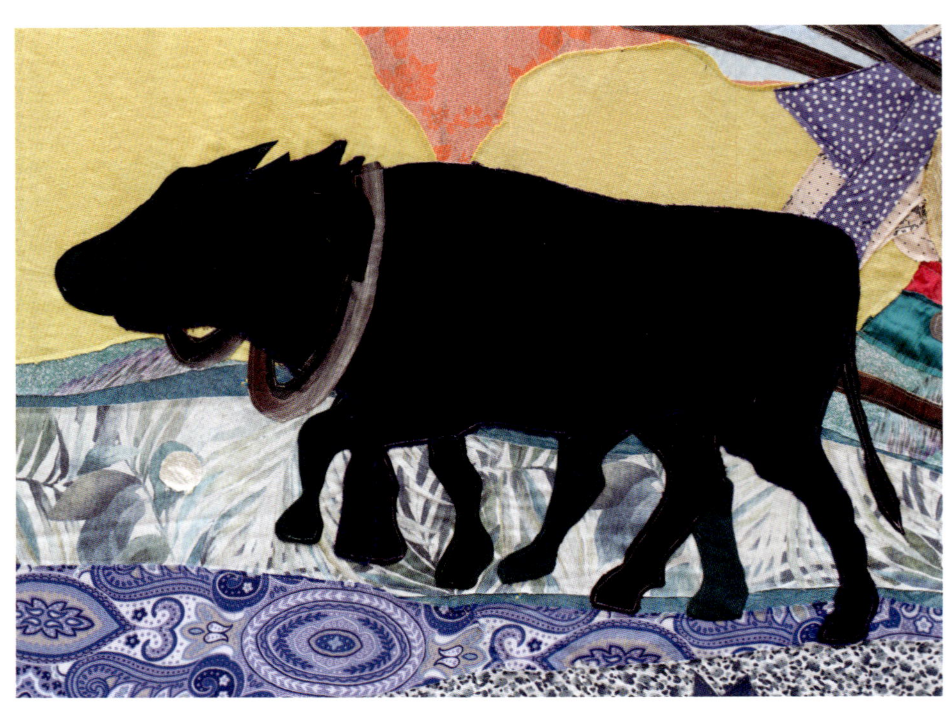

PREVIOUS, HERE AND OVERLEAF
Still on the Journey 2024
Acrylic paint and fabrics
on canvas
230 × 320

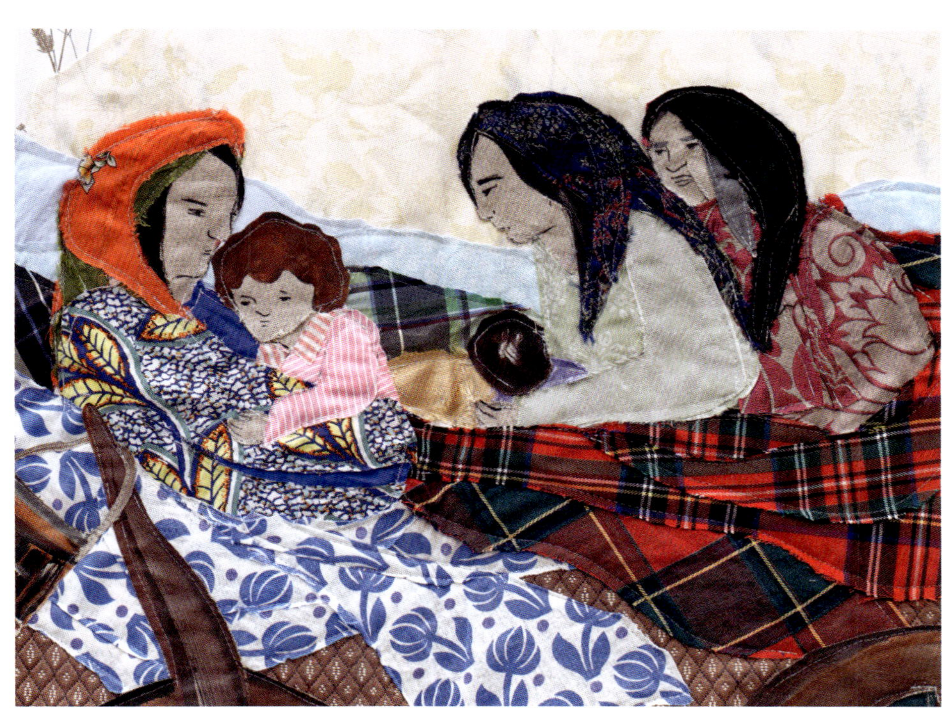

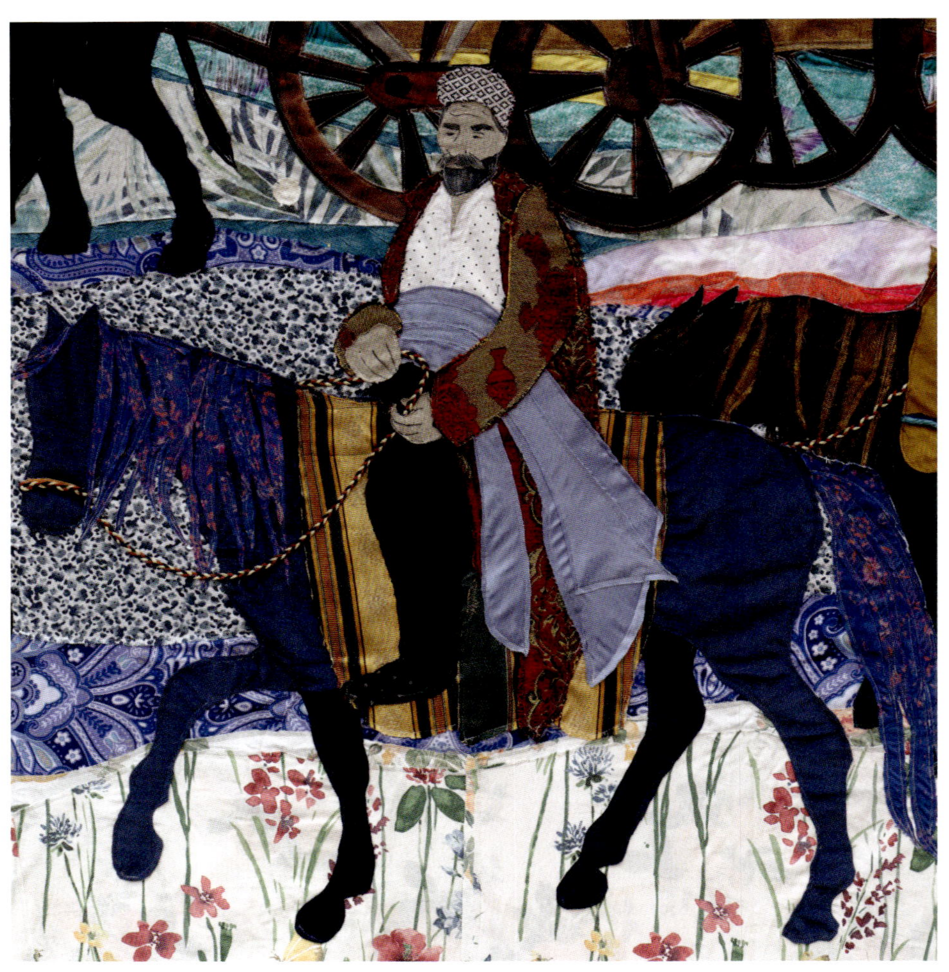

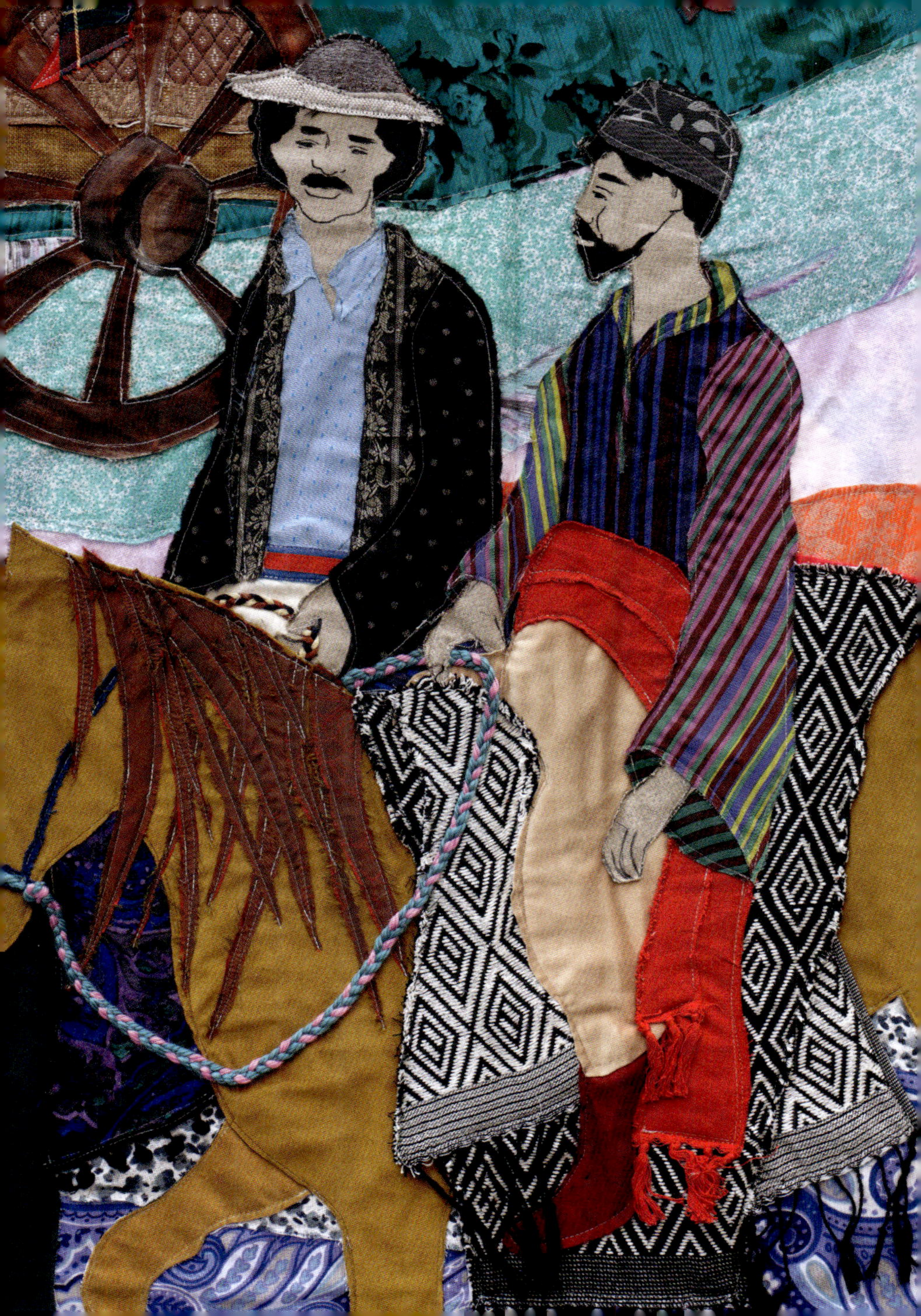

PUBLICNESS

Övül Ö. Durmuşoğlu

More than a millennium before Homer, a moon priestess in Mesopotamia named Enheduanna authored poetry. Her unique texts, written in cuneiform on tablets, are the earliest known example of first-person writing, though it took a very long time for scholars to credit her work. Other women took authorship in many ways from very early on, whether weaving on a board or working with a needle or chisel – a history in which Małgorzata Mirga-Tas claims a place for herself as a Romani woman with a needle. In a world of excessive images that repeat stereotypes consciously and unconsciously, she takes on the responsibility of creating living images of Romani communities to reshape the publicness of Romani wisdom and history through the medium of visuality.

'We have never been modern [and] no society has ever been primitive', writes the Brazilian anthropologist Eduardo Viveiros de Castro, before asking a straightforward rhetorical question: 'Then who is wrong, what needs explanation?'[5] Yet someone must always be coded as wrong in the binary construction of the 'universal', and that wrongness has been addressed in the most public manners. It is further manipulated and overwritten by those who hold the power of writing in their hands. Viveiros de Castro's question should not lead to a discussion of who is more 'modern' or more 'primitive'; it should spur us to find the critical power in the popular in order to respond to the collective consciousness and mould it further. The Romani community – the largest ethnic minority in the EU – has suffered. It is the necessity of finding a new public language for the Roma that forms a strong core in Mirga-Tas's works, as she seeks to address the artistic power of the popular in portraits and everyday scenes, and to turn the canons of visibility upside down.

Mirga-Tas's earliest public work was a carved wooden memorial honouring twenty-nine Romani people murdered in 1942 near the village of Borzęcin Dolny, east of Kraków, in 2011 (p.83). Then came *Wesiune Thana* (*Place in the Woods*), an installation set among the Romani houses in the Sądecki Ethnographic Park, an open-air museum of rural culture in Nowy Sącz, south-east of Kraków, comprising collages the artist made from stitched-together second-hand clothing and other textiles originating in the Romani communities she works with (opposite). As used clothes acquire a new life in the space of Mirga-Tas's scenes and portraits, they also enact

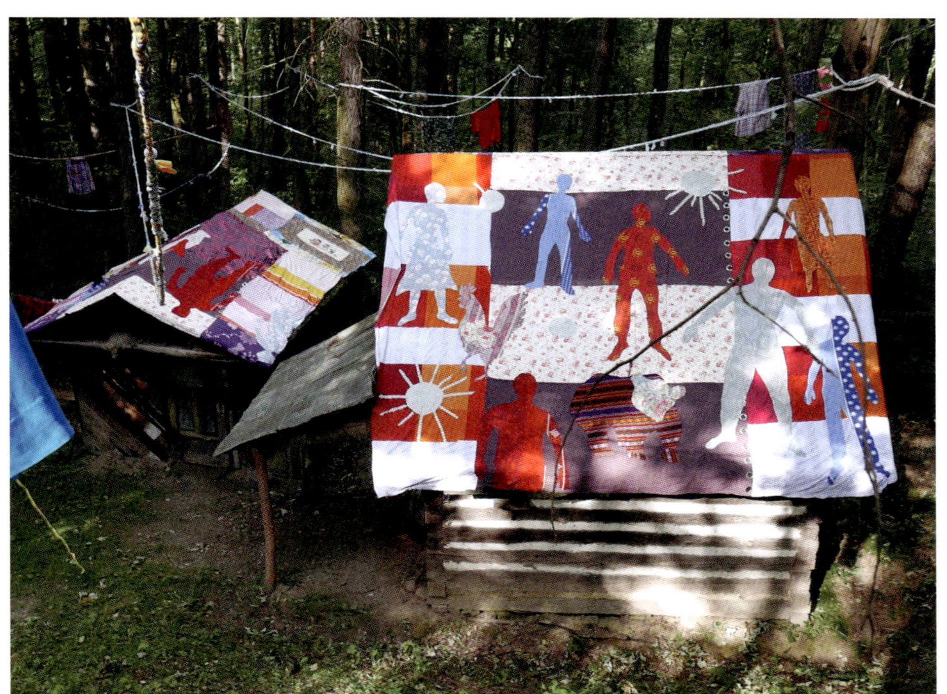

the living image of the Romani communities, adding to
the new public language built by their own authority.

Herstories 2019–21, which I co-commissioned with
Joanna Warsza for the 3rd Autostrada Biennale in Prizren,
Kosovo (2021), marked the public memory of the city in an
unforgettable way (pp.62–3). Here, Mirga-Tas showed large-
scale portraits of women from different Romani communities,
from Prizren to London, including women's rights advocate
Shpresa Agushi, community activist Nicoleta Bitu (p.80),
homemaker Zinet Galushi, artist Delaine Le Bas (p.63) and
singer and humanitarian worker Esma Redžepova (p.79).
Installed on a half-finished building on the Lumbardhi river
between the Romani neighbourhood and Prizren town centre,
Herstories marked the invisible distances the Roma continue
to experience in the city despite their strong cultural presence
in Kosovo. Like Enheduanna before her, Mirga-Tas continues
to show the way for future female authorships to proclaim
the equality, the freedom and the joy the Romani communities
have never ceased to have.

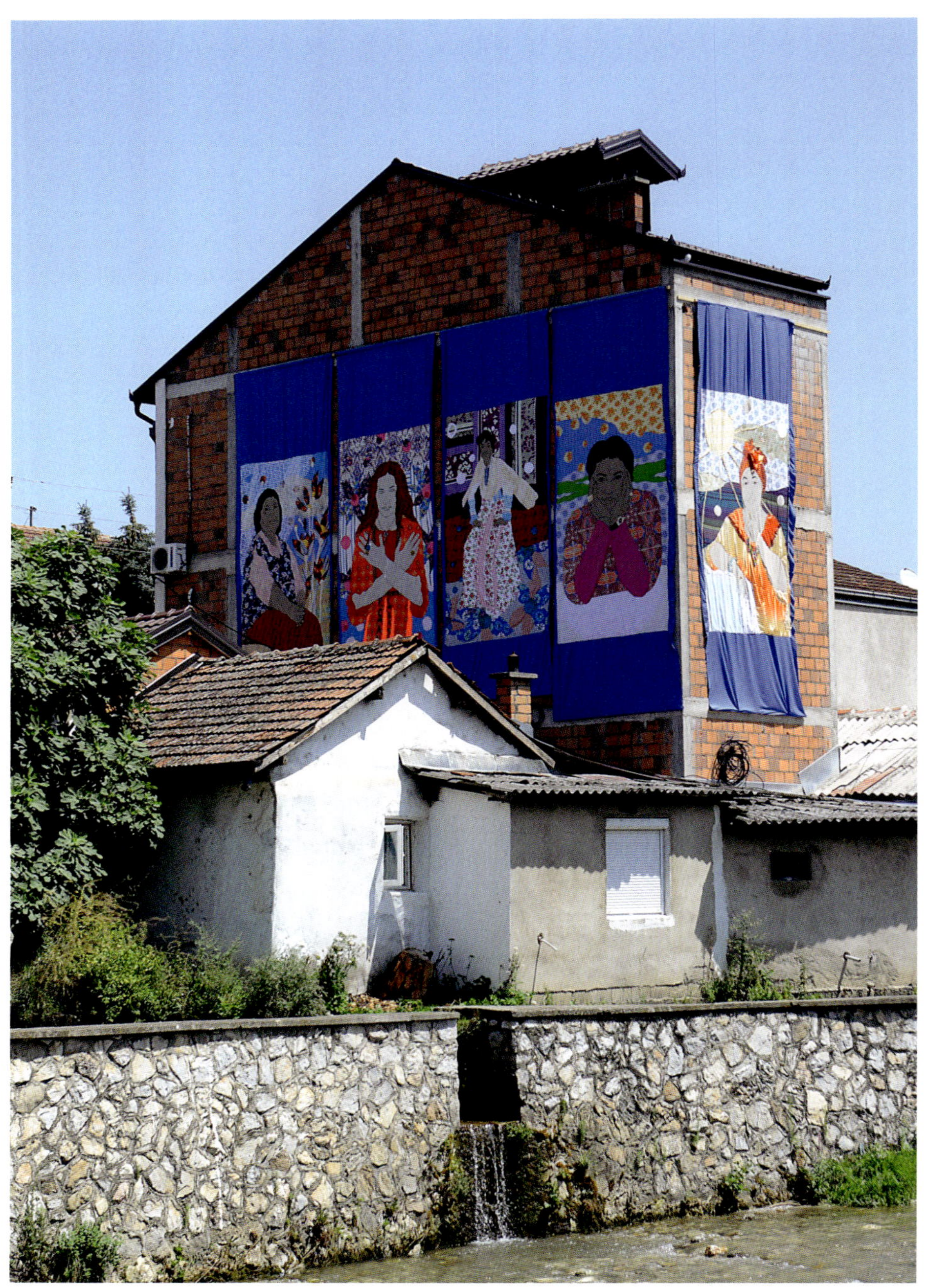

Herstories 2019–21
3rd Autostrada Biennale,
Prizren, Kosovo

Delaine Le Bas
from the series Herstories
2019–21
Fabrics, acrylic paint and
mixed media
385 × 211

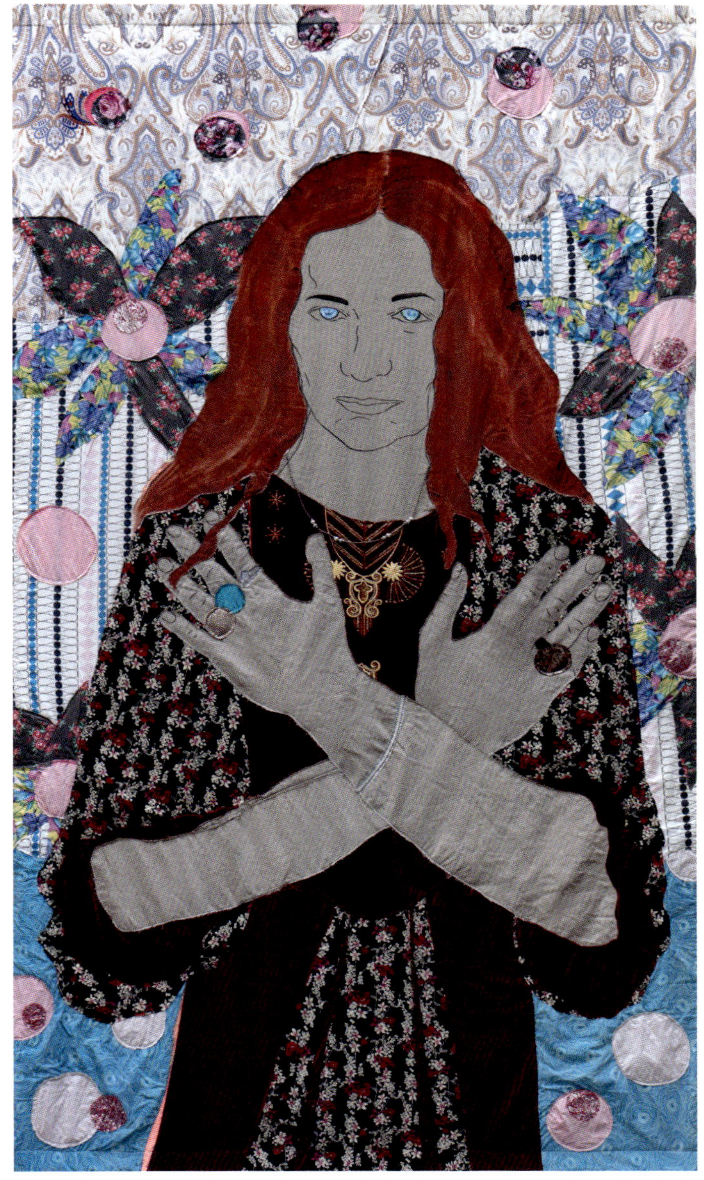

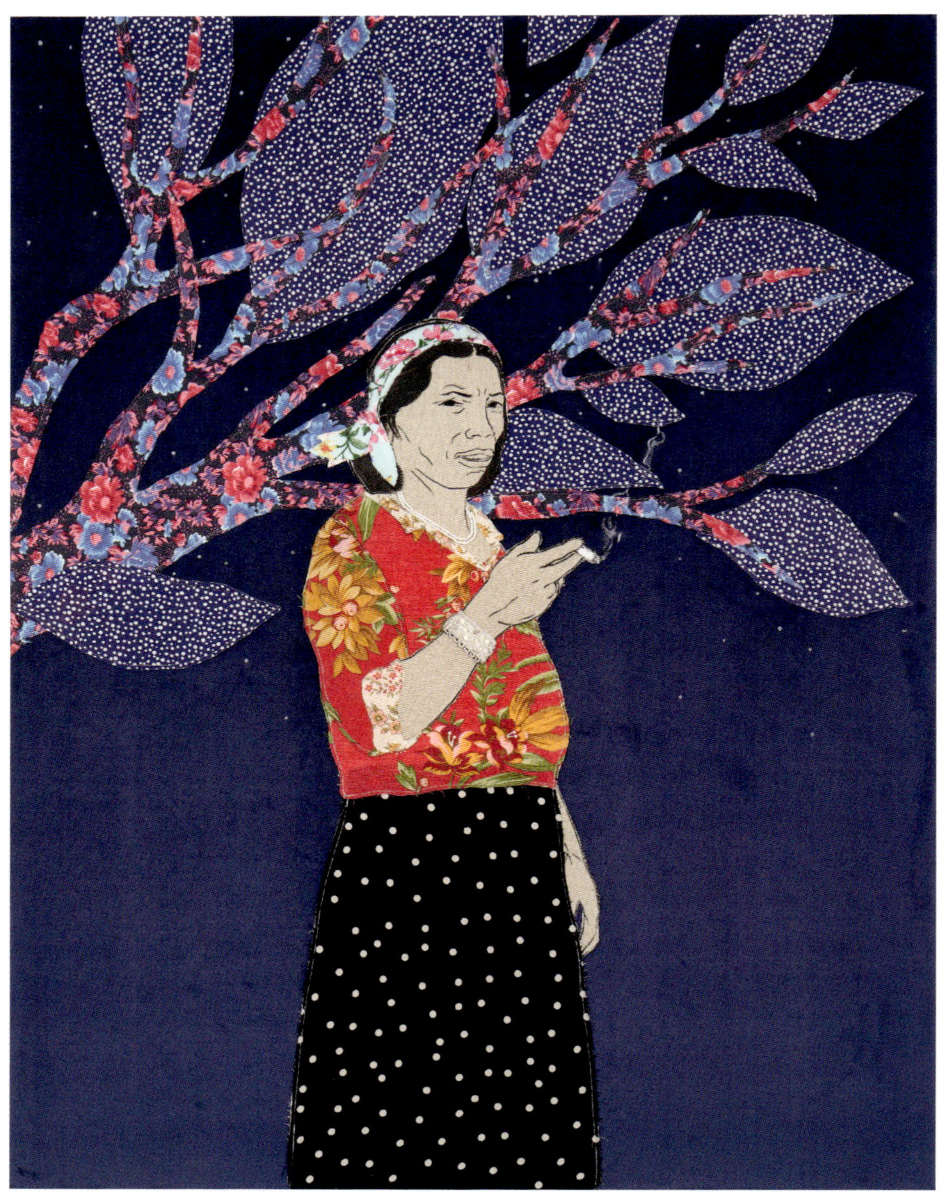

Romni 2023
Acrylic paint and fabrics
on canvas
128 × 99.5

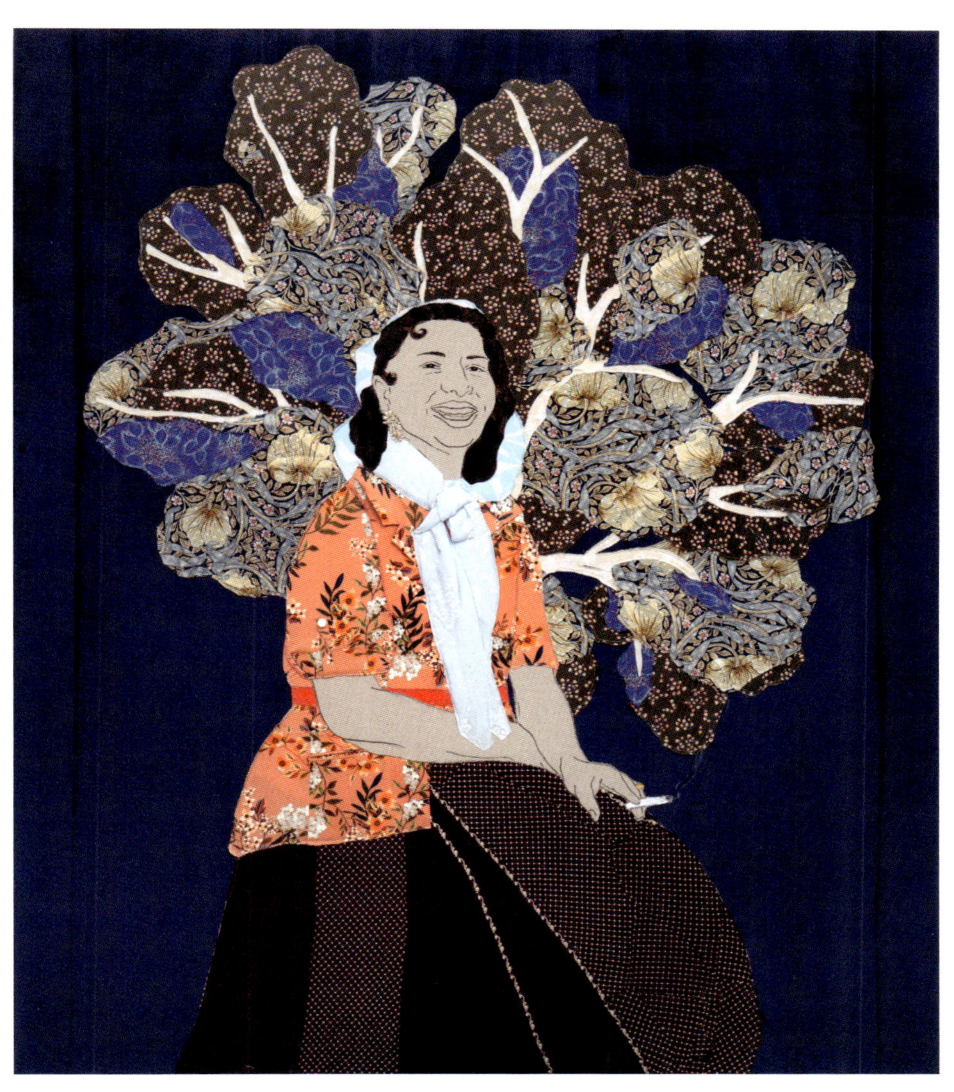

Sofia Taikon 2023
Acrylic paint and fabrics
on canvas
210 × 180

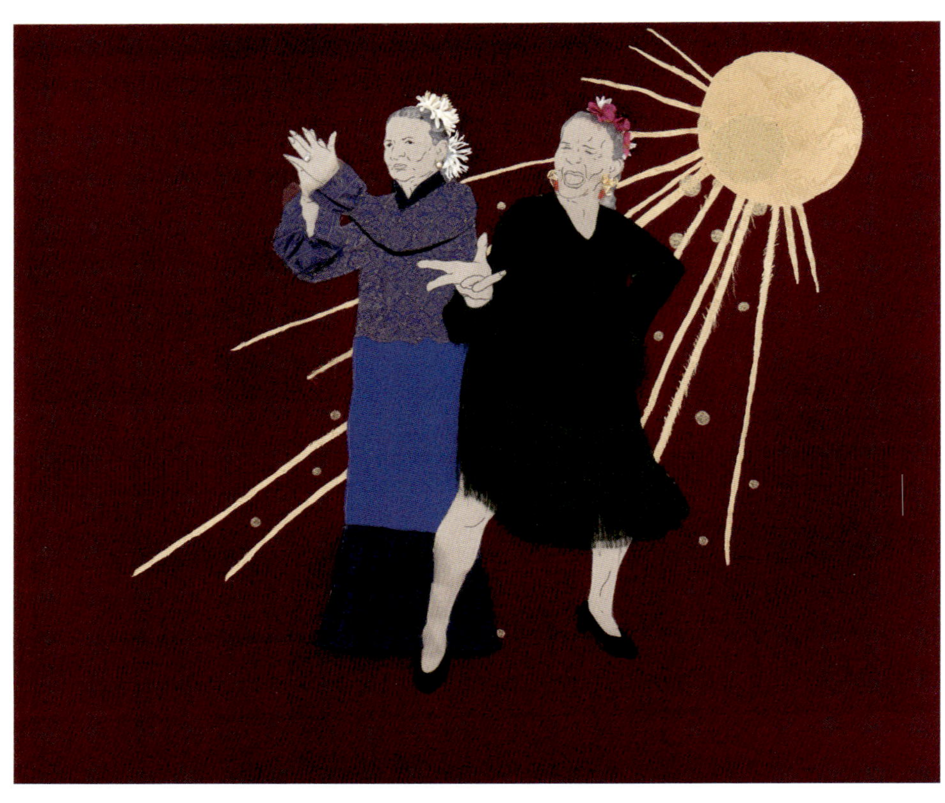

Herminia Borja 2023
Acrylic paint and fabrics
on canvas
265.5 × 323

Juana Vargas de las Heras,
"la Macarrona" 2023
Acrylic paint and fabrics
on canvas
266 × 309.5

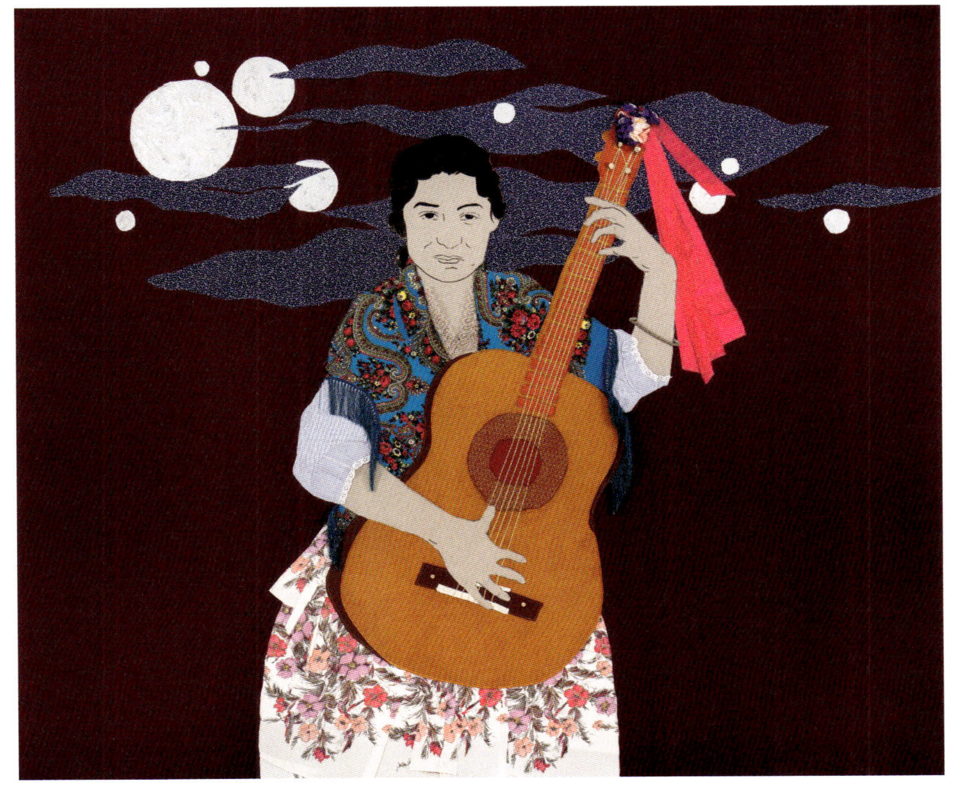

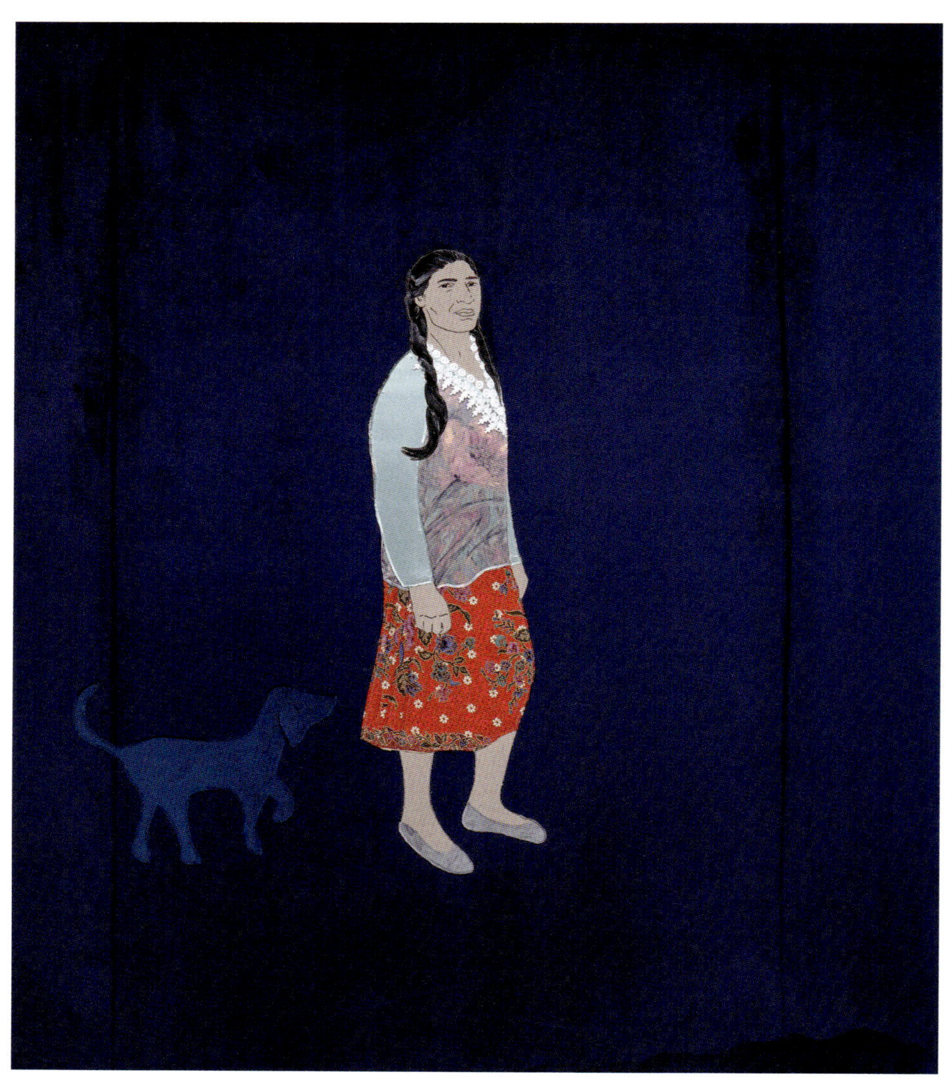

Wanda Siwak from the series
Siukar Manusia (Wonderful
People) 2022
Acrylic paint and fabrics
on canvas
270 × 260

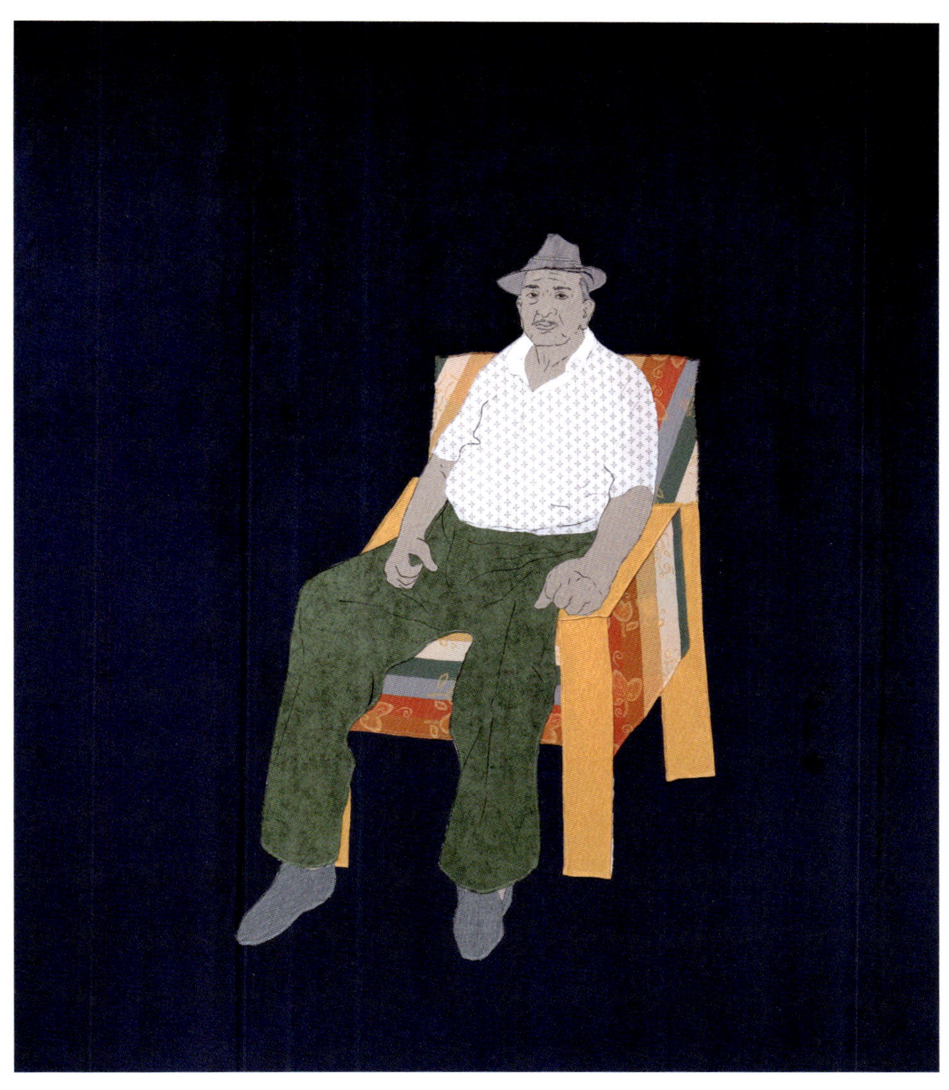

Edward Dunka from the series
Siukar Manusia (*Wonderful
People*) 2022
Acrylic paint and fabrics
on canvas
270 × 260

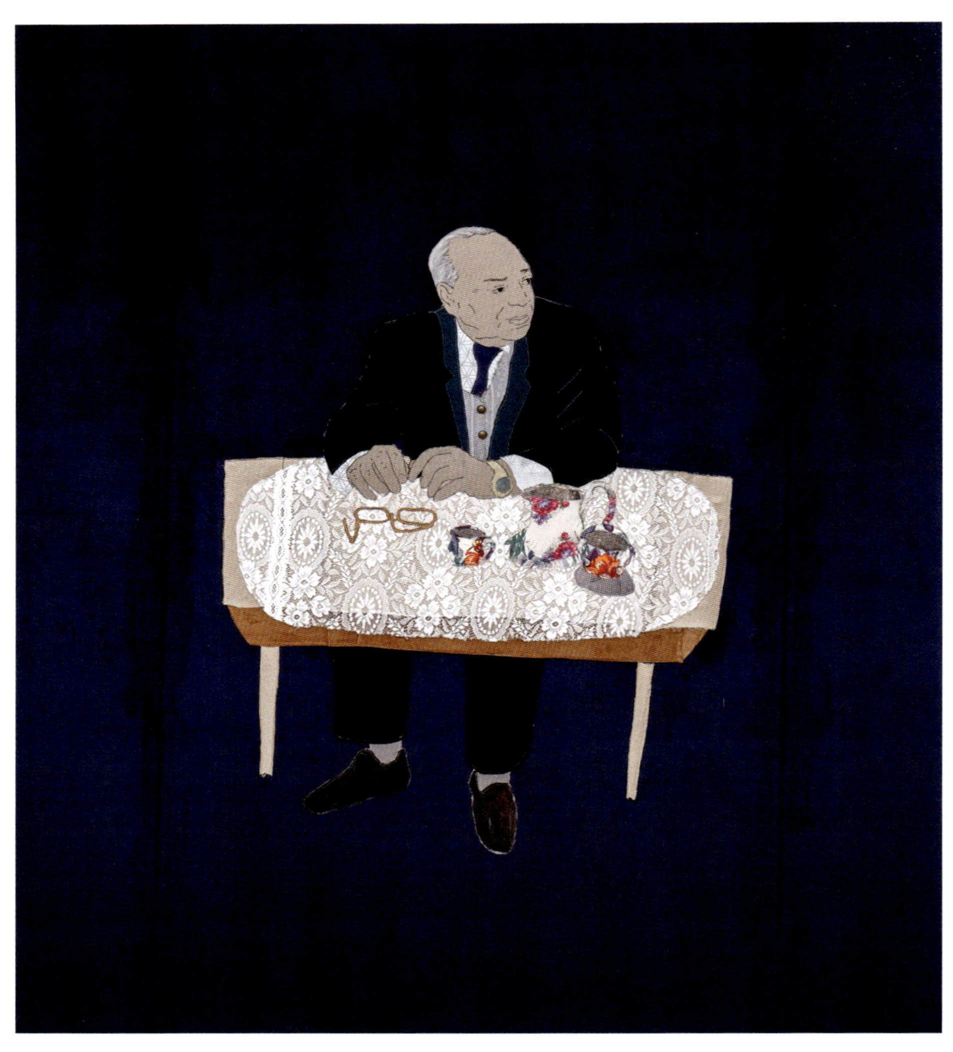

Marian Gil from the series
Siukar Manusia (*Wonderful
People*) 2022
Acrylic paint and fabrics
on canvas
270 × 260

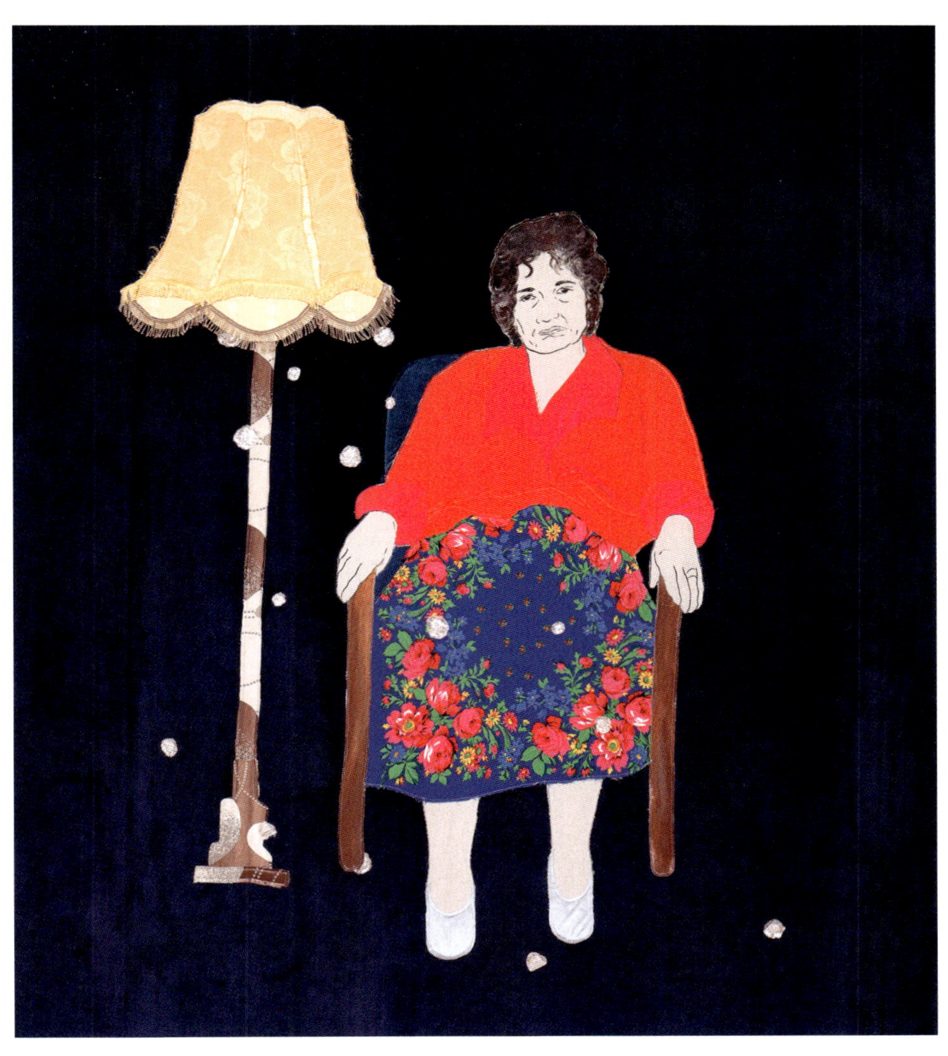

*Krystyna Gil from the series
Siukar Manusia (Wonderful
People) 2022*
Acrylic paint and fabrics
on canvas
270 × 260

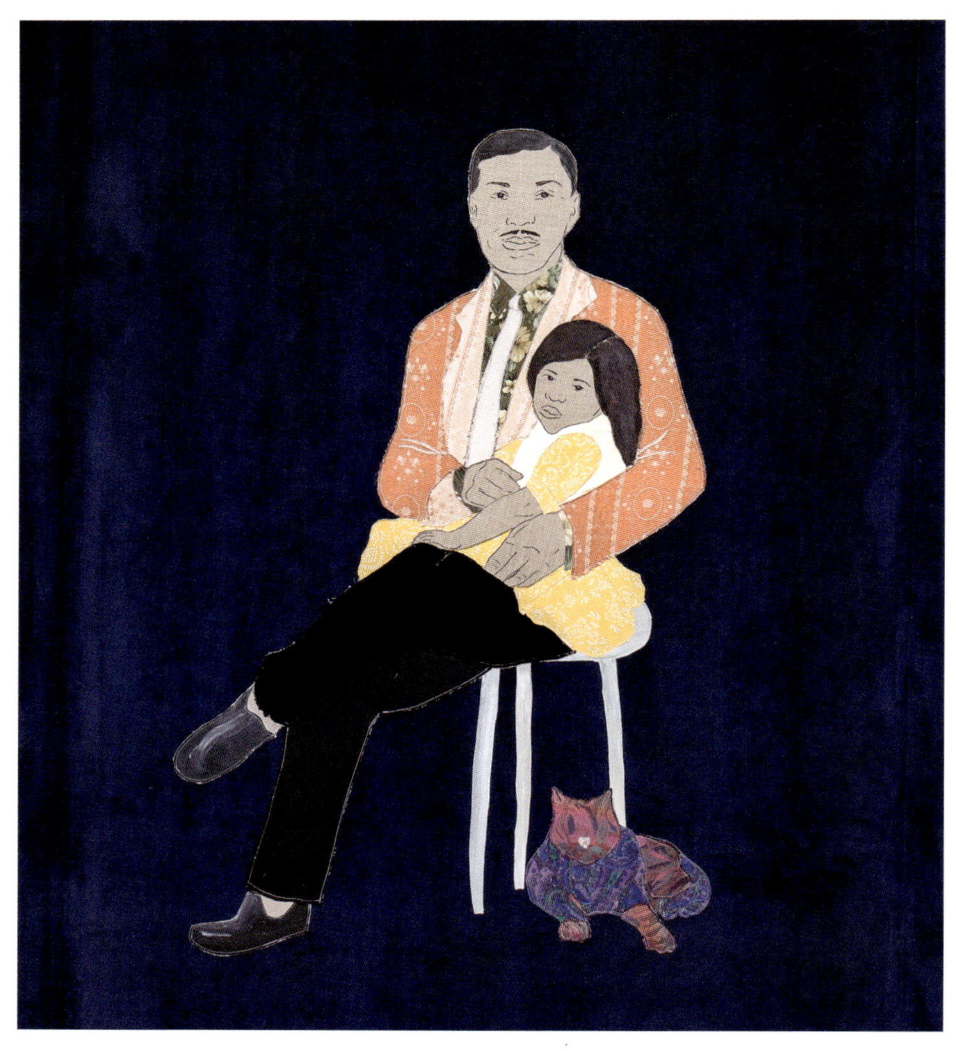

*Augustyn Gabor with his
daughter Elżbietą from
the series Siukar Manusia
(Wonderful People)* 2022
Acrylic paint and fabrics
on canvas
270 × 260

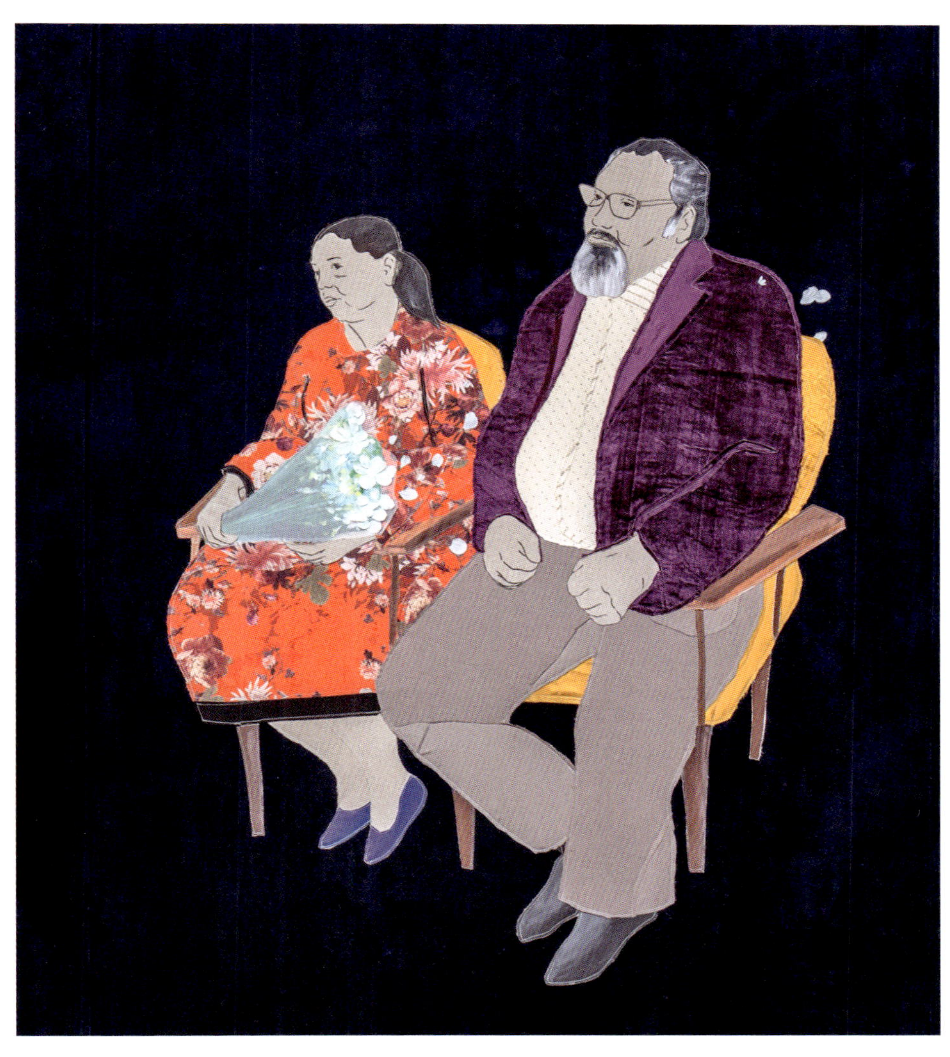

*Anna and Jan Gil from
the series Siukar Manusia
(Wonderful People)* 2022
Acrylic paint and fabrics
on canvas
270 × 260

IN CONVERSATION
MAŁGORZATA MIRGA-TAS & ANNE BARLOW

14 August 2024

ANNE BARLOW: Before we go into the concepts and themes of your work, I thought it would be nice for us to go back to the beginning. You have lived in the village of Czarna Góra since you were born. When was it that you knew you wanted to be an artist?

MAŁGORZATA MIRGA-TAS: I grew up in a Roma settlement, close to Zakopane. As a child, I never really thought about my future, only the present, and what I was going to do: go to the library, to school, to play with my cousins. But I was always doing something, and making things, sculptures with glue, different stones, or similar. My uncle worked at Jagiellonian University, and sometimes he visited with his students. They would give us pastels and pencils as gifts, and I began drawing often – but even then, I never thought that this would be a good profession for me. I always thought I'd be a different person, something else. Maybe even work in the library, which I loved. In high school I studied furniture design and then I turned to sculpture. For the Roma people, the word 'artist', at least when I grew up, did not exist. There were of course painters, and sculptors, other types of art professions, but not artists. For Roma, the word 'artist' was more abstract.

AB: This interest then led to your studying sculpture at the Academy of Fine Arts in Kraków. Can you describe, during those early years, how you experimented with the techniques of collage, and what eventually led you to work in textiles?

MMT: After leaving the Academy, we decided to move to Dublin. I was busy and didn't have time to work on my sculpture. But every day, I was drawing and then I started to cut up my clothes and add them to my work. I created collages with textiles, but also

paper. When I was back in Poland, I worked on a project with
Roma children about Nońcia (Alfreda Markowska). I asked
the children to collect clothes, and we used these clothes for
textile portraits of famous Romani people. That was the first
time I decided to sew a work, and I really enjoyed it, because
I worked with the children. Through art, I was able to teach
them about the Roma's story. A few years later, my friend
Wojciech Szymański invited me to work on a project in a forest,
Wesiune Thana (Place in the Woods) 2016 (p.61). I decided to dress
Romani houses from the 1960s, which had been moved to
this open-air museum in Malopolska. I covered the roofs with
fabrics showing characters and animals, warming them up and
adding colour. I started to think about the layering of materials;
the collages seemed more like sculptures in their composition.
It was always about the need to build something, maybe
because I studied sculpture.

AB: Which writers, artists or activists have been instrumental
or influential in your practice, and in what ways?

MMT: From an early age I was interested in The Harlem Renaissance,
which inspired me. In a way I envied this awakening and
the realisation that change is important and necessary.
The movement that was born among the African-American
community at that time still has an impact on Romani culture
and ideological transformation – the strive for change, and
the fight for human rights.

    After graduation, I naively thought that the whole world
was open to me, but this was not true, and I soon collided with
brutal reality. No one was interested in the subject of my work,
except ethnographic museums. I had to rethink my actions
and aspirations. I became an activist, which pushed me to
speak about important things through art. All my educational
projects were aimed at children and young people. Education
is important in creating a new generation with different ideals.

    Reaching for fabric was obvious, really. We all know the
tradition of creating patchworks in collective action. Women
would get together and sew quilts, curtains, bedding. Our
grandmothers, born before the Second World War, sewed
their own clothes with cousins and neighbours. It was ordinary,
simple work, but it was full of meaning. I turned to fabric at a
time when I could not carve. I started sewing from the clothes

we had at home, which, for sentimental reasons, we did not want to give to anyone. My mother gave me curtains, my sister gave me bedding, and so it began. Someone once told me that it's significant that minorities always use *tkanin* (fabrics) to say something about themselves. I think it's symbolic and important. The art of identity does not have to be relegated to the underworld. It can become part of contemporary practice and you should actually draw inspiration from your culture. It's always the artists of Romani origin that inspire me. They are the reason for my commitment and perseverance.

AB: You have spoken about the role of family and friends, but also the importance of animals. One of your works in this exhibition – *Familia (Family)* 2022 (p.32) – is an image of a bear. Could you speak about the symbolism of the bear?

MMT: An old Romani and Sinti profession originating in India was the training of wild animals. In Europe, the Roma trained a variety of animals but especially bears. For some, this is a traumatic history. But at the same time, bears were part of their life, part of the family, treated almost like children. The bears would sleep close to the house, they would work with families and live with them. People have a negative view of the Roma because of this, and I want to change this stereotypical vision; for people to understand the Roma's relationship with the bear, and understand that this was a moment in time. The Bergitka Roma, my community, have been in this area [Czarna Góra, at the foot of the Tatra Mountains] for almost 400 years. We are part of these mountains. And we can meet bears here, in the forest. For me, the bear is magic, and that's what I was thinking about as I started to sew *Familia*. I want to educate people about how to respect these animals. People, especially tourists, come into the forest and try to interact with them – they push them, try to take selfies. And they are surprised that bears hate selfies, and when they get angry, they attack.

AB: I'd like to talk about your visual source material, particularly your use of photography. You often use archival photographs, as well as your own photographs, as research material. Can you describe how you translate that source material into linear sketches and, from there, create compositions with multiple pieces of fabric?

MMT: I started thinking about archival photos a long time ago, after visiting two exhibitions of work by non-Romani artists. There were many photos of Romani people in the exhibitions, sometimes identified, sometimes not. They were continuing the age-old tradition of speaking about the Roma without consulting us. Later, I met an artist who asked me to explain how we celebrate holidays because she wanted to paint us. I said that she needed to talk with these people, go to stay with them, eat their breakfast, celebrate with them. But she didn't think she needed to. I started my own archive of photographs from my travels. I always ask people if I can photograph them and paint them, and I take note of their names. I want to show that these people are normal: they hang the laundry, they cook, they ride bikes, they sit in front of the house, they drink coffee. They are not dangerous, or different, or to be feared. By picturing the Roma in this way, showing the normality of their lives, I hope that others can learn to respect them, and that the Roma become visible in our country.

Early in my career, I also began to draw on the archive of my uncle, Andrzej Mirga, and to learn more about how the Roma have lived. I read many books which illustrated Romani people from the fifteenth century until the twentieth century. But these presented a stereotypical vision, and there were very few visuals or drawings created by Romani hands. So, I decided to change this, to give the Roma dignity, to talk about their stories. Of course, the women were of particular importance to me, because as a Romani woman, you grow up in a very patriarchal culture, where the men make decisions about your life, your future. But the women are amazing and are more progressive than the men. I don't think men like it when we talk about such things, and maybe they don't like me because of this work.

AB: It has been said that you approach the topic of Romani identity from a feminist perspective. And you have, in many instances, been drawn to certain female figures who have been important in terms of Romani culture, those that stand up for their community, for example political figures or survivors. You also collaborate often with other women.

MMT: In our patriarchal culture, the concept of feminism is abstract – at least, for the older generation, not for the younger as they can

be more independent. But for me it was different because
my family is matriarchal. My grandma was strong and made all
the decisions. And I have a lot of women cousins; we outnumber
the men in our community. A lot of us also don't have Romani
husbands, and this is a choice: to break away from tradition a
little. When I grew up, my father was very strict and wanted us
to know that there were special rules for the girls. He was always
telling us not to do things and telling my mother to check her
daughters. We couldn't go out at certain times, or talk to boys.
We couldn't speak Polish at home. Clothes were also important.
My father didn't like us to wear certain colours or earrings, for
example. I think he was trying to show us the ways to preserve
our culture, but at the same time, he decided how we were to
behave. We loved and respected our father, of course, but we
tried to explain to him that the world is different now. I think
the men don't think women can make decisions for themselves
about their lives. But I respect my culture. Rather than try to
change Romani traditions, we need to deal with them, making
little changes, and small evolutions – but we also need to
respect that there are rules.

AB: So as you say, it's not as simple as an act of resistance,
or rejection of a culture; it's more about evolving, adapting
and changing within it.

MMT: I respect the men in my community, but I try to tell them
that with my husband, it's more like a partnership. If I cook
something, he can also. If I'm cleaning the house, he can
help. It's not like in Romani culture where only the woman
does the cooking, while the man sits and waits. It's a different
relationship.

AB: It feels that what you have been describing is evident in the
presence of women in your work, in terms of communicating
their strength and personalities. One series that really struck
me was *Herstories* 2019–21, which was co-commissioned for the
Autostrada Biennale in Prizren, in Kosovo. Could you speak
more about those works and the people they relate to?

MMT: It was an amazing project, with a strong story about women.
My connection there was Edis Galushi; an activist from the
Roma settlement in Kosovo. I asked him to find me women

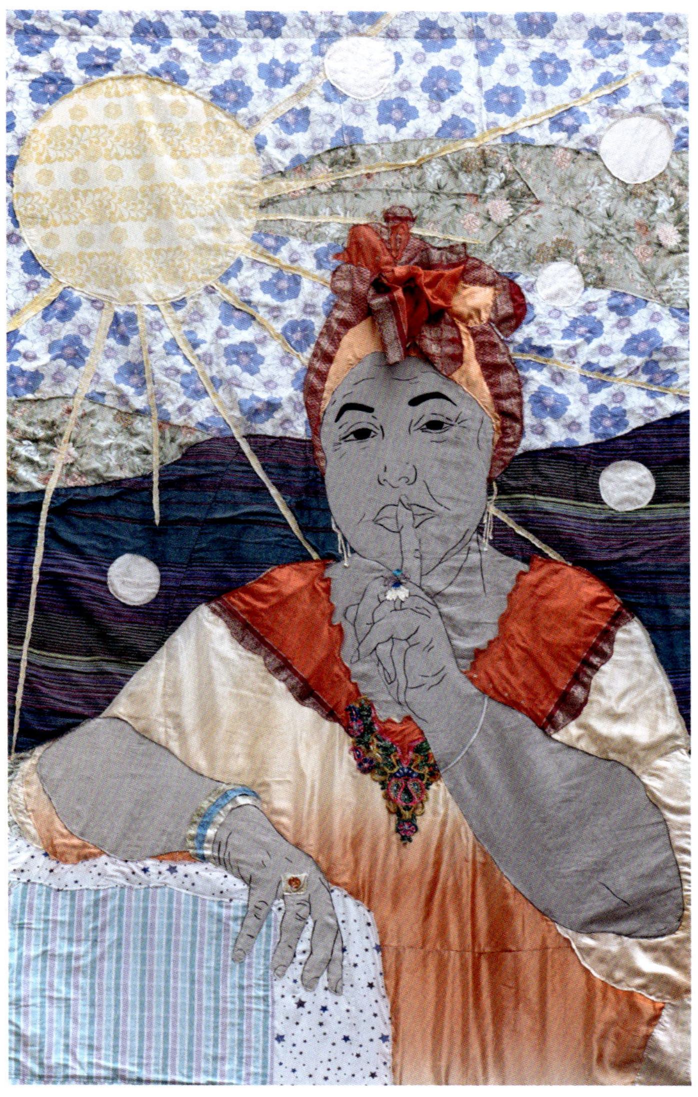

Esma Redžepova
from the series *Herstories*
2019–21
Fabrics and acrylic paint
381 × 213

Nicoleta Bitu
from the series *Herstories*
2019–21
Fabrics and acrylic paint
389 × 207

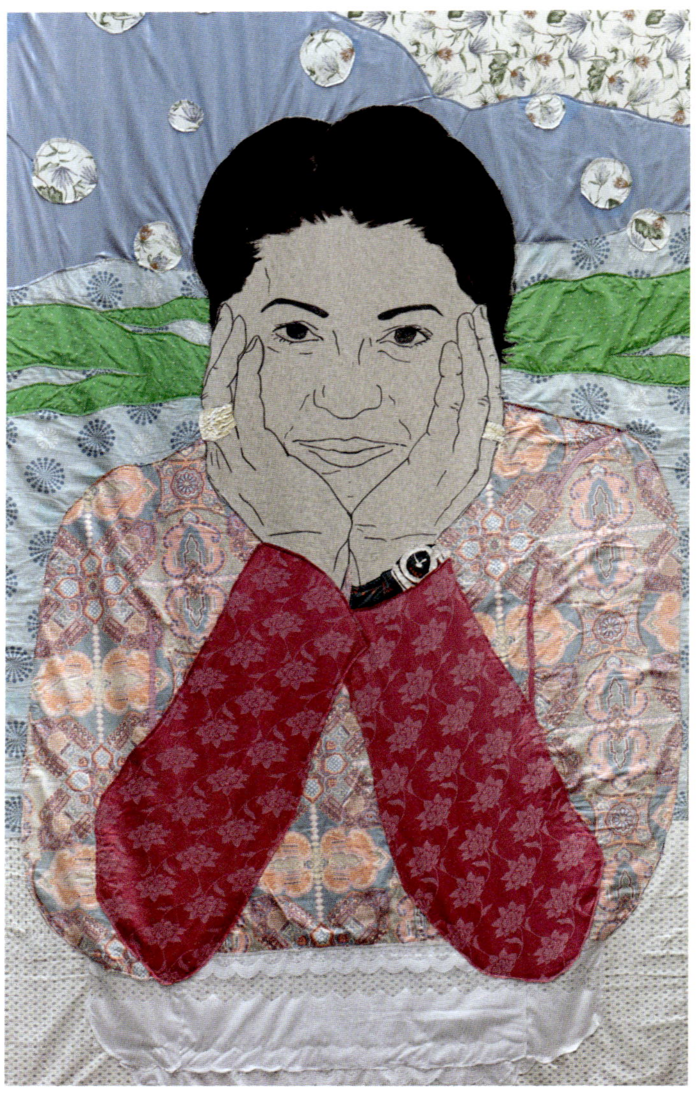

who are important for the Romani community there. A key example was Esma Redžepova, who everybody knows there: they call her Mama Esma, and she's a famous singer. I also asked Edis about his own story, and he told me about his mother, Zinet Galushi. She makes traditional wedding dresses for the Romani women who live in the settlement. I saw one of her dresses, and I met Edis's sisters. They were all very strong women, progressive, and very open – I think because of their mother. They told me she explained to them how life should look, how they should behave; to be more open and tolerant, regardless of tradition. And so, I decided to make a portrait of her. And then there was Shpresa Agushi who decided to create an organisation for Romani women who had been displaced and experienced terrible things during the war. Some of these women were raped and left with children, and their houses were also destroyed. The organisation was set up to help them and enable them to talk about what had happened. For the Roma, she's the strongest woman. She petitioned the Government and even enabled the passing of some laws to protect Romani women. She was a strong feminist and I think it's important to talk about her, and to celebrate her through my work.

There were more women who first agreed and wanted to be part of the project, but then they called to say that they were afraid of how people would react if they were to reveal themselves as Roma. These Romani women are brave but they were afraid that if they were pictured in the city, across these houses, they might be recognised and identified as Roma and might have trouble because of that. They want to be visible, but sometimes it's good not to be so visible. For me, it is sad that they were afraid to be pictured, but of course, I cancelled and told them not to worry, but that's why I think it was a very important project.

After the war, in Serbia they still do not accept Kosovo as a country. But when Kosovo was created, a Romani from Prizren was appointed the Minister for Culture. He came to the *Herstories* opening, and told me that he had never seen anything like this work.

AB: Some of this connects to another topic: the importance of memorialisation in your work, in relation to both historic and more recent events. In 2011, you made the sculpture,

Monument to the Memory of the Holocaust of the Romani, which was sited near Borzęcin Dolny, to commemorate twenty-nine people executed there in 1942. This was a sculpture made in wood, featuring silhouettes of a dying man and woman. It was later destroyed in what was deemed an act of anti-Roma violence. In response to that really violent act, you created 29. *Exercises in Ceroplastics* 2020 – incredibly poignant works made with pale pink wax and elements of the damaged epitaph. Can you speak more about that work and the choice of wax as a material?

MMT: When I think about the destroyed monument, and all the pieces that I found, I have many different feelings. The small bits of fragmented wood felt almost symbolic in a way, and made me think again about how such a thing could happen, and how these people could have been killed. I wanted to make something in commemoration of this, and to show that this can never happen again. Even though the original monument was destroyed, I think that each of the remaining broken pieces should be part of the memory.

I used wax because it is a part of our Romani culture: when somebody dies, candles are lit. And when the candles are almost burnt out, the wax goes deep into the ground, together with the coffin; it becomes part of our memory. I wanted the work to make a statement: to say 'never again'. You cannot kill us again, because we can speak out now, we're screaming, and we are stronger.

AB: Continuing with that subject matter, the 2022 portrait series *Siukar Manusia* (meaning 'wonderful people') depicts first-generation Romani inhabitants of the Nowa Huta district in eastern Kraków. These include Holocaust survivor and activist Krystyna Gil. Can you tell us more about these works as well as the rigorous research you have carried out, consulting sources such as audiovisual testimonies and archives such as the USC Shoah Foundation and Fortunoff Video Archive for Holocaust Testimonies?

MMT: When the International Cultural Centre in Kraków proposed an exhibition to me, I decided to show part of an ongoing project I was working on about Romani residents of Nowa Huta in Kraków, many of whom were survivors of the Romani

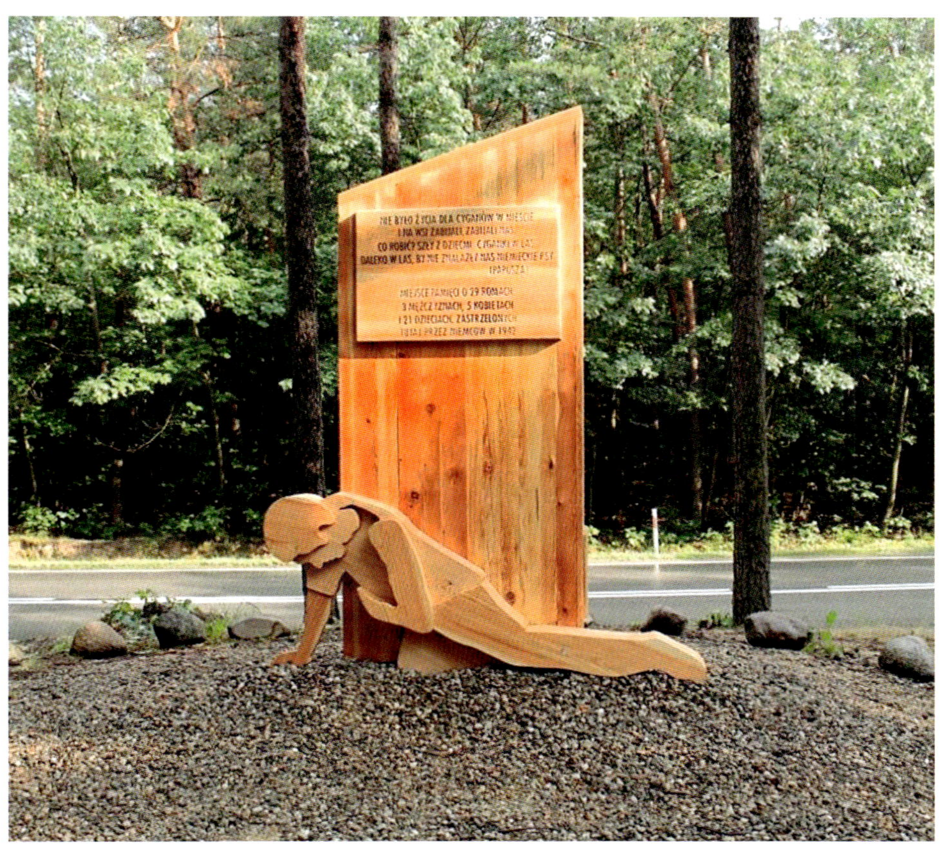

*Monument to the Memory of the
Holocaust of the Romani 2016
Wood (rebuilt after the
original sculpture from 2011
was destroyed)
Dimensions variable
Installation view on the site
of German Nazi crimes
during the Second World
War, Borzęcin Dolny,
Brzesko County, Poland*

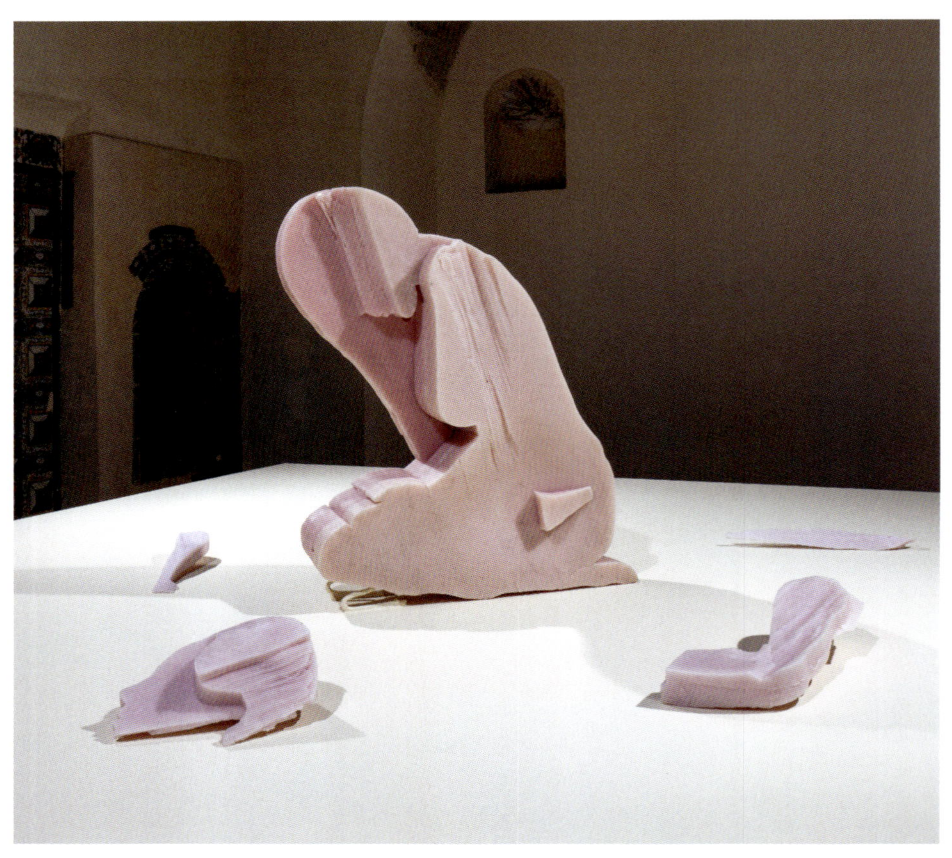

29. *Exercises in Ceroplastics* 2020
Paraffin wax and pigment
Dimensions variable
Installation view, *Małgorzata
Mirga-Tas: Remembrance and
Resignification* at the Centro An-
daluz de Arte Contemporáneo,
Seville, Spain, 2024

Holocaust. They came from small villages like mine, and they moved to Kraków because they wanted to survive; they had to work, and to improve the lives of their children. At the same time, it was not easy to be in a huge city, and to feel that nobody respects you or wants you there. But the survivors are strong, and it was really great to share this, even though it is a very tough story to tell. I often connect with the children of these people, and also activists who help me reach their families. They write to me, and send me many photos from their own archives. They sometimes ask me to show them in a particular dress, or a particular way. I was so happy to connect with one man, Edward Dunka, who is still alive. Edward lived in Germany, but he came to Kraków, and he was crying with his wife. He was so pleased that somebody shared the story, because they have endured many bad situations, yet nobody knows this, or talks about the fact that Nowa Huta is a Romani area. So that's why this project was very special.

AB: I'd like to move to something quite different now: your references to art history. You often reappropriate and reimagine historical artworks that have typically presented Romani identity in negative ways, instead creating affirmative imagery of Romani individuals and communities. The Lorraine engraver Jacques Callot has been a particularly important reference. In response to seeing his etchings depicting Romani people, you made a series of large format textiles called *Out of Egypt* in 2021 (p.43). It brings to mind this idea of the journey, and travelling, which can also be seen in the works in the exhibition *Dromeskri zuta (On the Journey)* and *Still on the Journey* 2024 (pp.48–59). Can you elaborate on how you approached Callot's compositions, in terms of deciding which components to use, or adapt, and why?

MMT: As you say, this is about reappropriation. When I talk with my friends, we are happy that there are these images out there, but Jacques Callot's drawings are not nice: they show us as very dirty people, doing bad things such as stealing. His work continued to portray a stereotypical view of Romani people, anti-Gypsy, and very negative. My initial feeling about Callot's images was that I wanted to colour them and change the people's clothes. These may be Roma from the fifteenth and sixteenth centuries, but they had normal clothes, and they were not dirty, nor without dignity. And so, I set about adding colour to them. At first, I thought I would do this by painting, and then I felt I needed to sew a tapestry and use clothes from my family. I began to use many things from my house and from my mother, as well as some second-hand clothing, to give them more energy. I like to use the same compositions as Callot, but vary the people in each, sometimes lifting people from multiple images and putting them together in one scene.

When I research, I am interested in what museums have in their archives relating to the Roma and Sinti. Sometimes these are beautiful graphics or paintings without stereotypical depictions, painted by non-Romani hands. But most of them are the same repeated scenes, from the sixteenth century almost to the twentieth century. If you look at images of the Roma wandering from Hungary and of Roma wandering from France, the Romani families are shown exactly the same way. Typical copies, which have not changed over the centuries. I am very curious why, for the artists who drew them, there was nothing else interesting in our culture. Of course, there are portraits of Romani women, without names, without dignity, often naked, treated as exotic objects, often sexual objects. This touches and saddens me. We are always an object for someone. In my work, I fight to give us back our subjectivity, to give us dignity and finally allow us to speak with our own voice.

In France, in the sixteenth century, it was even legal to kill Romani people; people were allowed to hunt us or use us as slaves. At the time, Callot was making fun of this in his drawings; it was like a joke. When I first showed *Out of Egypt*, one woman posted on the internet complaining that I ought to respect these amazing French artists, and that I was failing to understand that times were different, that this was more like satire. I wasn't sure how to respond. It was shocking to see not only how people represent us, but that they think they know us better than we know ourselves – that they can say more about our culture than we can. I try to portray us in a more positive way. But at the same time, it's hard. The story of the Romani victims is complex. Did you know there were enslaved Romani people in Romania into the nineteenth century?

AB: You have created two monumental new works specifically for the Tate St Ives exhibition. What were the influences for these two new works, and can you speak about your thought processes behind their development?

MMT: I knew right away that I wanted to show Romani women who have never been identified by name, but only used as an interesting exotic image. Looking at portraits of Romani women in various archives before 1900, I came across some photos, as usual without names – they were simply called 'Romani women' or 'Gypsies' – and of course, they were mostly from the ethnographic section. Delving into their history – or rather the lack of history – I decided to pay homage and respect to them. One work I have referenced, *Young Gypsies* 1879 by the French painter and classicist William-Adolphe Bouguereau, shows a young Romani woman with a child. Another image entitled *Spain: Gypsies* (c.1860–80) shows two Andalusian Romani women, in beautiful clothes, captured in a moment of conversation, a banal scene. What caught my attention was this quote from a website offering it as a print for sale:

> This captivating image transports you to a bygone era, offering a glimpse into the rich cultural history of Spain through the eyes of these two Gypsy women. With their expressive gazes and traditional attire, this photograph is a stunning addition to any home or office, evoking a sense of wonder and intrigue.

Unfair, inaccurate and sometimes violent imagery of the Roma continues to be shared. There often is no opportunity to oppose such views; unfortunately, they do not give us the chance to speak for ourselves. For me, the new works are not only intended to be beautiful scenes; they are about reclaiming the images of these women, their respect and dignity, and continuing the theme of *Herstories*, which is ultimately about the visibility of women. These images reject their subjection and tell us more about them; that they are not just part of an exotic decoration.

AB: The exhibition includes three acrylic paint and fabric works recently acquired for the Tate collection – *The Three Graces* 2021 (p.6), and *Miri Daj (My Mother)* (pp.22–3) and *Side Thawenca (Sewn with Threads)* (pp.24–5), both 2019, which are on floor-standing screens. Another work installed on a screen is *Untitled (After Gentile da Fabriano)* 2023 (p.26) but in this case it is hung on a wall so that you cannot see its rich burgundy surface on the reverse. What was it about this screen format that interested

you, and can you speak more about the Gentile da Fabriano
piece, also as that has a direct art historical reference to da
Fabriano's *Adoration of the Magi* from 1423 (p.27)?

MMT: For *The Three Graces*, I worked with my uncle, Andrzej Mirga,
and we decided to sew a work based on photos from his
archive, mostly from the 1970s and 80s. He went to one village,
Szaflary, which has one of the biggest Romani settlements
in the area, and we also have family that live there. I selected
a few photos of people I knew or who were from the closest
family and have long since passed away. *The Three Graces* tells
the story of a relationship of wonderful women, of friendship
and respect. The screen *Miri Daj (My Mother)* was shown at
the 11th Berlin Biennale (2020). There were three screens
showing my grandma, my mother, and my mother's older
cousin. The story is about generations of strong women. My
grandma is a survivor of the Second World War; she has lived
under Communist rule for almost all her life. My mother is
from another, younger generation, but she also grew up in a
Communist society. I wanted to show the generational trauma
of their times, but simultaneously, how to be strong, how to
change your life, and how to survive. My mother is shown
sitting outside her house. This was the first time I had sewn on
to a screen like this, so you can see a view from the front and
also a view from the back (pp.22–3). And I painted part of it
as well.

For me, screens have a special meaning. They are supposed
to give the space where they are located warmth and intimacy.
And the images on them have a certain magical power, or
spirituality. My mother is shown from two sides, giving the
impression that she is with you in the place where the screen is.

I'm the third generation and I grew up under Communist
rule too, of course – until the time of Solidarity (Solidarność).
I was maybe twelve years old, or perhaps older. I remember
when we queued outside shops, only to find there was nothing
on the shelves. But I was happy; as children we didn't really
know what was going on. We just thought it was normal to
have very little.

AB: Representing Poland at the Venice Biennale in 2022 with the
project *Re-enchanting the World* must have been a very significant
moment. The work (pp.10–11, 17) takes inspiration from

The Hall of the Months, late fifteenth century allegorical frescoes at the Palazzo Schifanoia in Ferrara, Italy (p.16). When you first visited Ferrara in 2021, what were your reactions to seeing this? And how did you develop your ideas about your own work in terms of the reference to both the composition and content – an example of which can be seen in the work *June*, which has been kindly lent to this exhibition by the Museum of Modern Art in Warsaw?

MMT: This project is probably the biggest of my life. When I visited Ferrara, I was really surprised by the richness of the lapis lazuli; the frescoes were very impressive. I wanted to create something based on them and settled on using the same structure of frames. I didn't want to illustrate a mythological story in the same way, but I did want my story to take place across a single year, to speak to the passing of time, and to make use of the zodiac signs. I decided to focus on my heritage, and asked my whole family, even those who live in different places, to send me images from their archives. They were keen to be involved and sent me a lot of photographs – and clothes – from when they grew up.

In the third band of the Ferrara frescoes, people from the seventeenth century are depicted. And I wanted to do the same, to illustrate the normal lives of Romani people from my village, from my family. I thought this would be easy to do but it was hard to decide which photos to use, to obtain the necessary permissions, to identify who was in the photos, what they were doing, and so on. It was a long process. I wanted to be sure that everyone was happy to share their stories and to be part of the project. The project represents a number of women from *Herstories*, but there are also men – friends, uncles, my husband.

AB: How did you feel that audiences responded to this work?

MMT: I think the response was generally very positive, actually. It was really all about the Romani people for me. It was them that I was thinking about when I was sewing this in my studio, for five months, every day. I'm always thinking about the need to continue my work, to share the Romani story; to let people know that the Roma exist, and that they deserve to be more visible. As a community, we want to change the stereotypical views of ourselves. I often wonder what the Romani people think about all this, and the presentation at the Pavilion. But when they came for the opening, they were crying, and it was so emotional. Even now, every time they repeat the film about the Pavilion on Polish television, my mother cries, as do my aunt and cousins. Because we don't have our place in this world; we don't have our own country as such – even though we grew up in Poland I still sometimes feel that I don't belong, that I'm not a part of the culture in this country. When we opened the Polish Pavilion, the Romani people said, 'This is our house.' They felt they were part of something for the first time; that it was their Pavilion – not a Polish Pavilion, but a Romani Pavilion. They immediately recognised the amazing women from their own countries, but they were also able to identify with and relate to my family story – they could see their own aunt, parents, children.

AB: You are careful to point out that you identify as Bergitka Roma (mountain community), a specific Romani group, and at the same time, your work relates to the wider, transnational communities of Romani people. To what degree are projects such as *Wesiune thana (Place in the Woods)* 2016 a critique of how museums represent 'folk culture' or situate particular communities within an ethnographic context?

MMT: Things have changed a lot, but it's still difficult to move beyond the ethnographic context. When I finished at the Academy of Fine Arts, the first proposal I received was from an ethnography museum. I felt that I needed to continue my work, everything that I'm doing, and to share my identity, but also the wider story of the Roma, and the many problems that we have. But at the same time, I'm an artist, and I want to be considered as such, for my work, my skill, my experiences. My artist friends and I wonder how it has not been possible for us to talk about our identity, our culture. We know everything there is to know, yet we have been mostly excluded from the mainstream art world. In the past, non-Roma were invited to make exhibitions on Romani identity and Romani culture. Now we have our own voice and they cannot marginalise us. There are non-Romani artists who, as they say, have taken a liking to the Roma and want to talk about us, because we are so colourful. I understand people who live close to our community, who live with us, but

I do not understand people for whom this is a current topic, a hot topic from which they can quickly get out. For us, what we are is not a disguise, it is not a role for a moment, but our whole lives. Who we are defines us and we cannot suddenly become other people. There are some Romani organisations, for instance, the European Roma Institute for Arts and Culture (ERIAC) in Berlin, that have explored how the Romani community is part of this bigger story. And we should talk about that – we need to.

AB: Your focus on Romani-oriented residencies and programmes really reflects the strength of your commitment to supporting and deepening connections among Romani practitioners. I wondered if you could speak more about the Foundation Jaw Dikh! that you established in Czarna Góra to promote and preserve Romani culture and identity, and what it has led to in terms of artistic projects and activism?

MMT: We opened the Foundation in 2015. Initially it was only intended to encourage artistic projects for Romani children. And then, one day, I decided to make it a Romani residency for Romani artists, because I was really encouraged by what they were doing and thinking about. I wanted to share experiences with them, and to become friends, to open up meaningful dialogue and to establish connections. Now, the residencies are not only for Romani artists, but most applications are from the Roma. This year I decided to invite young artists, in high school or not long out of it, to join more established artists. It was a great opportunity for the younger artists to mix with those that were more experienced, and the younger artists feel invested. They help us to build a strategy. My husband Marcin and I work together on the Foundation and now we have all kinds of artistic projects, but also more political ones, on a range of topics. For example, when the war in Ukraine began, my cousin, who works in Kraków, devised a project for the Ukrainian children and people. But the focus is only ever on Romani culture and identity. We're building a leadership strategy for the Romani people.

NOTES

1. Éva Kovács, 'Fekete testek, fehér testek' (Black bodies, white bodies), *Beszélő* (Speaker), vol.14, no.1, Jan. 2009.

2. Quoted in 'The Recognition of the Nazi Genocide of the Sinti and Roma', *European Holocaust Memorial Day for Sinti and Roma*, https://www.roma-sinti-holocaust-memorial-day.eu/recognition/the-recognition-of-the-nazi-genocide-of-the-sinti-and-roma, accessed 26 Aug. 2024.

3. Silvia Federici, 'How the Demonization of "Gossip" Is Used to Break Women's Solidarity: Gender oppression shaped the notion of "idle women's talk."', in *In These Times*, 31 January 2019: https://inthesetimes.com/article/the-subversive-feminist-power-of-gossip, accessed 26 Aug. 2024.

4. bell hooks, *Yearning: Race, Gender, and Cultural Politics*, Boston, MA 2014 p.15.

5. Eduardo Viveiros de Castro, 'Cosmologies: Perspectivism', in *Cosmological Perspectivism in Amazonia and Elsewhere*, Manchester 2012, p.61.

FURTHER READING

The list begins with titles that focus specifically on the work of Małgorzata Mirga-Tas, and continues with more general books about Romani history, art and culture.

Stina Edblom (ed.), *Małgorzata Mirga-Tas: I Have A Dream | Suno Mangi Działać | Jag Har en Dröm*, Göteborg 2023.

Wojciech Szymański and Joanna Warsza (eds.), *Małgorzata Mirga-Tas: Re-enchanting the World*, Berlin and Warsaw 2022.

Wojciech Szymański and Natalia Żak (eds.), *Małgorzata Mirga-Tas: Travelling Images*, Kraków 2022.

Ariella Aïsha Azoulay, *Potential History: Unlearning Imperialism*, London 2019.

Thomas M. Buchsbaum and Sławomir Kapralski, *Beyond the Roma Holocaust: From Resistance to Mobilisation*, Kraków 2017.

Silvia Federici, *Re-enchanting the World: Feminism and the Politics of the Commons*, Oakland, CA 2018.

Tímea Junghaus and Katalin Székely (eds.), *Paradise Lost: The First Roma Pavilion, La Biennale di Venezia 2007*, London, Munich and New York 2007.

Anna Mirga-Kruszelnicka, Esteban Acuña C. and Piotr Trojański (eds.), *Education for Remembrance of the Roma Genocide: Scholarship, Commemoration and the Role of Youth*, Kraków 2015.

Lucy Orta (ed.), *Mapping the Invisible: EU-Roma Gypsies*, London 2010.

Nicholas Saul and Susan Tebbutt (eds.), *Role of the Romanies: Images and Counter Images of 'Gypsies'/Romanies in European Cultures*, Liverpool 2004.

Daniel A. Baker and Maria Hlavajova (eds.), *We Roma: A Critical Reader in Contemporary Art*, Utrecht 2013.

First published 2024 by order of the Tate Trustees
by Tate Publishing, a division of Tate Enterprises Ltd,
Millbank, London SW1P 4RG
www.tate.org.uk/publishing

Published on the occasion of the exhibition

Małgorzata Mirga-Tas
Tate St Ives
19 October 2024 – 5 January 2025

The Whitworth, The University of Manchester
11 April – 7 September 2025

Małgorzata Mirga-Tas is organised by Tate St Ives in
collaboration with the Whitworth

with support from

The Małgorzata Mirga-Tas Exhibition Supporters Circle:
The Polish Cultural Institute in London
Frith Street Gallery, London

and Tate Members

A catalogue record for this book is available from
the British Library

ISBN 978 1 84976 965 5

Distributed in the United States and Canada
by ABRAMS, New York

Library of Congress Control Number applied for

Senior Editor: Emma Poulter
Production and picture research: Bill Jones
Designed by Astrid Stavro Studio
Colour reproduction by DL Imaging, London
Printed and bound by Gomer Press, UK

Measurements of artworks are given in
centimetres, height before width and depth.

Where they exist, original Romani titles of artworks
are provided, followed by their English translation.

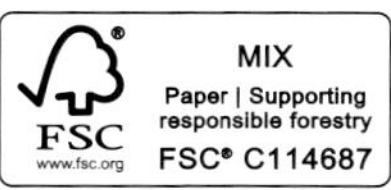

Cover: *Roma Pasio Peskro Khier (Roma in Front of
the House)* 2024 (detail, see pp.35–7)
Frontispiece: *June* from *Re-enchanting the World* 2022
(detail, see pp.10–11)
Page 4: *March* from *Re-enchanting the World* 2022
(detail)

ABOUT THE AUTHORS
Anne Barlow is Director at Tate St Ives.

Katarzyna Depta-Garapich is an artist and
researcher working across various media including
sculpture, performative gestures and video, site-
specific installations and drawing. Her recent body
of work explores mythmaking in family storytelling
positioned within the debate around the ecological
and ethical issues resulting from the impact of
humans on nature.

Övül Ö. Durmuşoğlu is a Berlin-based curator, writer
and educator working on constructive critiques of
civilisation, sustainability of intersectional futures
and practices of togetherness. She co-leads the Art
in Discourse programme at the HBK Braunschweig
University of Arts, Germany.

Giles Jackson is Curator, Interpretation at Tate
St Ives.

Timea Junghaus is an art historian and
contemporary art curator of Romani origin. Since
2017, she has served as Director of the Berlin-based
European Roma Institute for Arts and Culture.

Wojciech Szymański is is an art historian and
art critic, independent curator and editor. He is
currently assistant professor at the Institute of
Art History at the University of Warsaw, Poland.
He co-curated Małgorzata Mirga-Tas's exhibition
Re-enchanting the World at the 59th Venice Biennale
in 2022, and co-edited the publication *Małgorzata
Mirga-Tas: Re-enchanting the World*, Berlin and
Warsaw 2022.